**The Daily Telegraph
Friday 26 July:**

Iron Lady Stands Strong

"We did not fight two World Wars to defend Europe from dictatorship and oppression just to hand it over to the next tyrant bent on world dominance!"

The British Prime Minister, Margaret Thatcher, lived up to her nickname as 'The Iron Lady' today. Echoing Winston Churchill, the British leader during World War Two, she delivered a strong speech in parliament condemning the Soviet Union's demands and vowing that Britain would resist aggression in Europe "with every last breath".

**Daily Mail
Tuesday 30 July:**

Today the British Prime Minister, Margaret Thatcher, informed the nation that the British Army was on a full war footing and ready to fight. She stated that the territorial army and reservists have been mobilised and most have joined their units, and that regular army units in Germany are at full war-time strength and on full alert, prepared for any eventuality.

**The Guardian
Sunday 4 August:**

Britain At War!

This morning at 4am the Soviet Army crossed the border into West Germany. The Prime Minister responded with a declaration of war in a fiery speech in an emergency session in parliament.

So far there has been no news on the progress of the fighting, although there are reports of many German towns being bombed or hit by rockets. At present there are no reports of nuclear weapons being used. When asked about the likelihood of a nuclear response, Thatcher replied, 'Britain will

**Daily Mirror
Tuesday 6 August:**

British Troops Holding the Line!

Our reporters in Germany tell us that the British troops holding the West German border against the Soviet invasion are holding their ground and refusing to budge, despite heavy Soviet attacks throughout the last three days.

The RAF has been striking deep into East Germany, attacking airfields and troop convoys. These attacks have been successful in keeping the Soviet Air Force

AF324284

IT'S 1985 AND THE COLD WAR JUST GOT HOT!

Team Yankee is a complete set of rules for playing World War III Wargames.

Based on the book written by Harold Coyle in 1987, Team Yankee brings the conflict that simmered throughout the Cold War to life. You will command your troops in miniature on a realistic battlefield.

In Team Yankee, a heavy combat team of M1 Abrams tanks and M113 armoured personnel carriers faces a Soviet invasion of West Germany. Outnumbered and outgunned, Captain Sean Bannon and his men will have to fight hard and they'll have to fight smart if they are going to survive.

Lt. Colonel Yuri Potecknov's motor rifle battalion is preparing to execute its mission in the scientific manner that he had been taught at the Frunze Military Academy and used in Afghanistan. Victory today will bring the world proletarian revolution that much closer.

Find out more at:
WWW.TEAM-YANKEE.COM

IRON MAIDEN

BRITISH ARMY IN WORLD WAR III

Written by: Phil Yates
Editors: Peter Simunovich, John-Paul Brisigotti
Graphic Design: Sean Goodison, Casey Davies
Stories by: Harold Coyle, Jennifer Ellis
Proof Readers: David Adlam, Mark Goddard, Tim Harris, Sean Ireland,
Michael McSwiney, Luke Parsonage, Stephen Smith, Garry Wait
Miniatures Design: Evan Allen, Tim Adcock, Matt Bickley, Will Jayne

Cover Art and Illustrations: Vincent Wai
Miniatures Painting: Aaron Mathie
Web Support: James Brown
Playtest Groups: Dad's Army (Gavin Van Rossum),
Northern Battle Gamers (Nigel Slater).
Wardogs Hannover (Kai Bergemann)

CONTENTS

All rights reserved. No part of this publication may be reproduced, stored in a retrieval system, or transmitted, in any form or by any means without the prior written permission of the publisher, nor be otherwise circulated in any form of binding or cover other than that in which it is published and without a similar condition being imposed on the subsequent purchaser.

© Copyright Battlefront Miniatures Ltd., 2016. ISBN: 9780994120694

BAOR
BRITISH ARMY OF THE RHINE
BRITISH ARMY OF THE RHINE
Lübeck
Hamburg
LANDJUT
XXXX
NORTHAG
Wilhelmshaven
Bremerhaven
Oldenburg
Weser River
1ST
NETHERLANDS
CORPS
2ND
GUARDS
TANK
ARMY
Bremen
Elbe River
XXX
Aller River
Elbe-Seiten Canal
1ST
GERMAN
CORPS
3RD
SHOCK
ARMY
XXX
Midland Canal
Hannover
To the Rhur
Teutoburger Wald
Weser River
1ST
BRITISH
CORPS
Leine River
Brunswick
Magdeburg
XXX
1ST
BELGIAN
CORPS
NORTHAG
Harz Mountains
XXXX
CENTAG
3RD
GERMAN
CORPS
Kassel
8TH
GUARDS
ARMY

When World War III broke out in August 1985, the British Army Of the Rhine (BAOR) had been defending the West on the border between West Germany and East Germany for just over forty years. These soldiers, the third generation of British soldiers to stand watch on the North German Plain, quickly proved their mettle.

The Second World War ended with Germany divided into four parts, each under the control of one of the victorious powers: Great Britain, France, the United States, and the Soviet Union. As the rivalry between East and West heated up, this division became permanent. The three western powers formed the Federal Republic of Germany (FRG), known as West Germany, while the Soviet Union formed the German Democratic Republic (GDR), known as East Germany, to rule their part.

The political divide was matched by a military divide with the western powers forming NATO (the North Atlantic Treaty Organisation) and the Soviet Union forming the Warsaw Pact to coordinate with the Soviet states of eastern Europe. NATO divided responsibility for the defence of Germany into three army groups. The northernmost, NORTHAG, the descendant of Field Marshall Montgomery's victorious 21st Army Group from the Second World War, was a multi-national force under the command of the BAOR (British Army Of the Rhine).

NORTHAG was tasked with defending the North German Plain between the Harz Mountains and the North Sea. This looked to be the most likely path for a major Soviet thrust to the west. Although deemed ideal tank country in the Second World War, the whole plain was broken up by a series of rivers running northwards to the sea. The British had found these to be unexpectedly troublesome when attacking eastwards towards the Elbe River, and confidently expected the Soviet Army to find them equally troublesome when attacking westward towards Germany's western border on the Rhine River.

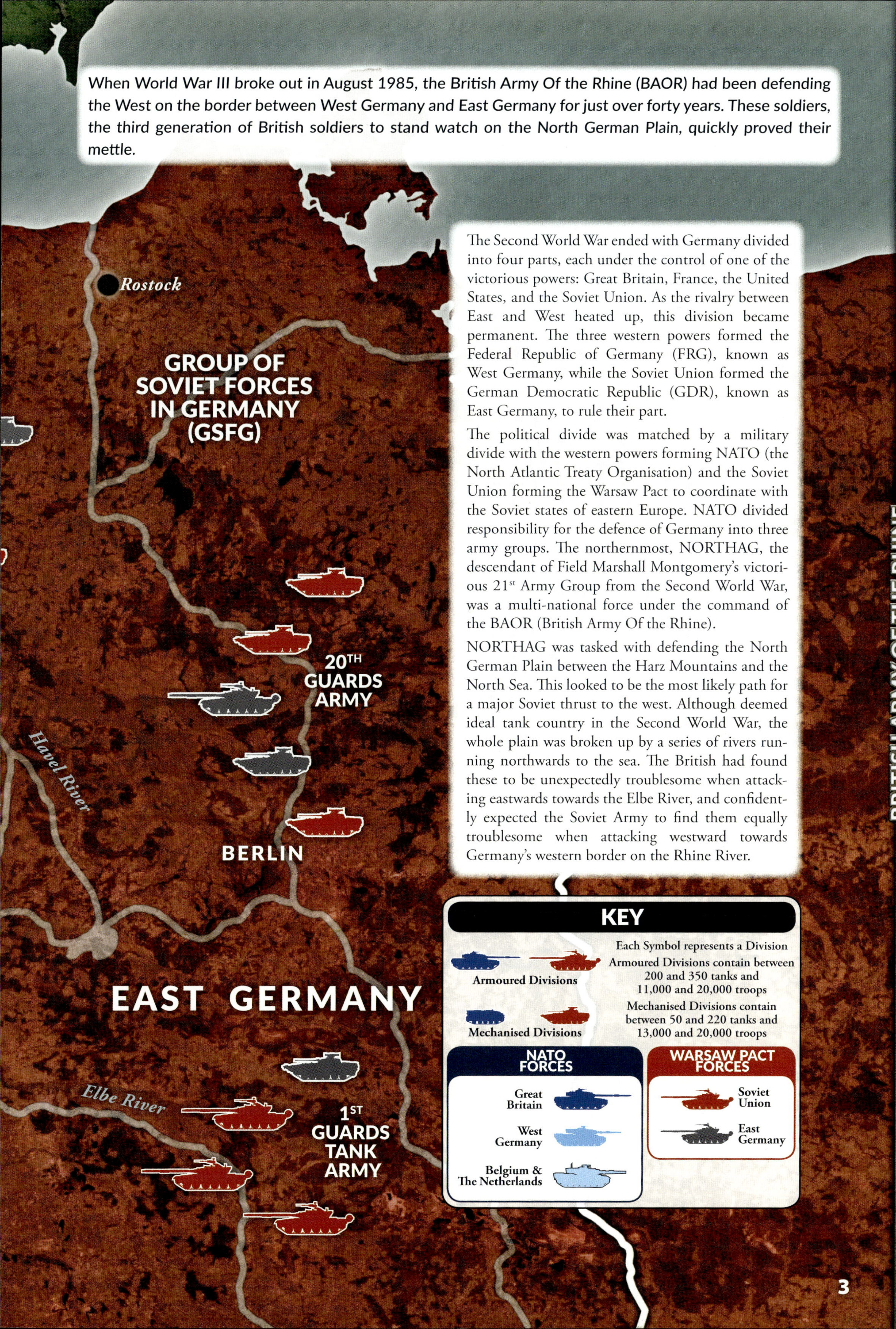

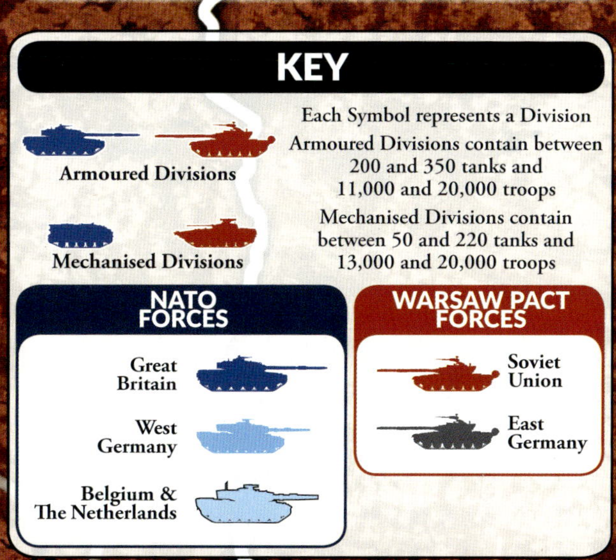

To further complicate matters for an attacker, the German population had increased since the Second World War and the rural villages had expanded creating a network of defensible areas each separated from its neighbour by just a few kilometres. The commanders of NORTHAG hoped to use the network of towns and villages to slow the Soviet advance and then the river lines to stop them cold.

When the war began on 4 August 1985, The British forces in NORTHAG consisted of 1st British Corps defending Hannover and 2nd British Corps being hastily formed as the NORTHAG reserve. 1st British Corps contained Britain's three Armoured Divisions and the 2nd Infantry Division which had been stationed in Britain until mobilisation just weeks before.

Even as 1st British Corps was being brought up to full strength, a second corps, 2nd British Corps, was in the process of forming from the regular and territorial brigades stationed throughout the British Isles. Only the first of these new divisions had reached Germany when the war began, but over the following days several more were rushed to the front, just in time as it turned out.

The pre-war British Army was a small, highly-trained professional force. Its experiences in Northern Ireland during the Troubles and in the Falklands War of 1982 had both shown it to be effective, and revealed problems that needed to be addressed. By 1985, the Army was as ready for what would come as it could be.

Facing 1st British Corps was the Soviet 3rd Shock Army of four tank divisions and one motor rifle division. Its main role, as predicted by pre-war intelligence, was to thrust westward through Hannover, the main crossing point on the Leine River, then cross the Weser to reach the Rhur, the industrial heartland of West Germany, on the Rhine River. A simultaneous thrust along the boundary between NORTHAG and CENTAG (the Central Army Group) was expected to shatter the small 1st Belgian Corps, then turn northwards to slash across the British rear areas.

While this was taking place, the plan called for the 2nd Guards Tank Army to break through on the boundary between 1st Netherlands Corps and 1st German Corps, thrusting west to link up with an airborne landing at Bremen while encircling the German corps from the north.

To a degree, the Soviet plan worked. The Netherlands delayed in mobilising their army, hoping for a diplomatic solution to the situation. Thus weakened, they were unable to stop the 2nd Guards Army's thrust. Within a week the remainder of the 1st Netherlands Corps had been pushed back out of Germany and their own northern provinces. Reinforced by 2nd British Corps, they still held a line on the Maas River. After the failure of a lone battalion of the British Parachute Regiment to hold the crossing at Arnhem on the Lower Rhine River, the key to the defence was the city of Nijmegen and its bridges. Meanwhile, the 1st German Corps had fallen back to the Teutoburger Wald covering the northern flank of the 1st British Corps, linking them with 2nd British Corps to the west.

To the south, the 1st Belgian Corps had been switched to CENTAG, and with reinforcement from the 5th US Corps, was still containing the Soviet thrust in the rough terrain of the Harz Mountains.

For 1st British Corps, it had been a tough fight. Initially their covering forces, then their main force had been forced to give ground, slowly retreating to the Leine River. A Soviet heliborne landing in an unexpected location had disrupted the defence, forcing the abandonment of Hannover, and a further retreat to the Weser River line. So far, that line was holding.

The climax of the first stage of the war came on the 14 August. At dawn, furious Soviet attacks pushed across the Maas, through the Teutoburger Wald and across the Weser, only to be halted by desperate fighting after gains of less than 20 km (12 miles). The next day, the newly-arrived 3rd US Corps, flown across the Atlantic to join up with their pre-positioned equipment, spearheaded a counterattack towards Wilhelmshaven, seeking to cut off the Soviet spearhead. Simultaneous counterattacks by CENTAG to the south heralded a new phase of the war. The great retreat was over.

3RD ARMOURED DIVISION

As Britain's 3rd Armoured Division, 'The Iron Division', moved into position south of Hannover, the atmosphere was a strange mix of familiar deployment exercises and the tension of the unknown to come.

The division's role as I British Corps reserve formation and the knowledge that the 1st and 4th Armoured Divisions would take the brunt of the first Soviet thrust exacerbated the unreality of the situation. The sense of being on just another exercise was heightened by the need to integrate the Queen's Dragoon Guards (QDG), their reconnaissance regiment, and the 19th Infantry Brigade as they arrived from England.

With such a wide frontage for two divisions to hold, it was not a matter of if, but when the Soviets would breach the line and force the forward divisions to fall back to the main line of defence on the Leine River.

The first battlegroups of the Third Armoured Division were ordered forward on the night of 6 August, with Scorpion and Scimitars of A Squadron, the Queen's Dragoon Guards making contact with a Soviet forward detachment around midday on 7 August.

Breaking contact after giving the Soviets a bloody nose, the covering force retired behind the 17th/21st Lancers at Schellerten where the leading Soviet battalion also took a pounding. While the fighting continued at Schellerten, the Irish Guards (IG) battlegroups launched counterattacks to recover the bridges at Heinde that a Soviet air assault had taken, and stop a thrust aimed at the autobahn at Rhüden. It was the support of the airmobile Gordon Highlanders landing from Lynx helicopters that finally allowed them to halt the Soviet advance.

With the success of the airmobile Light Infantry at Sehnde in the north allowed the 4th Armoured Division's cut off 11th Armoured Brigade to withdraw through Hannover, avoiding encirclement and destruction.

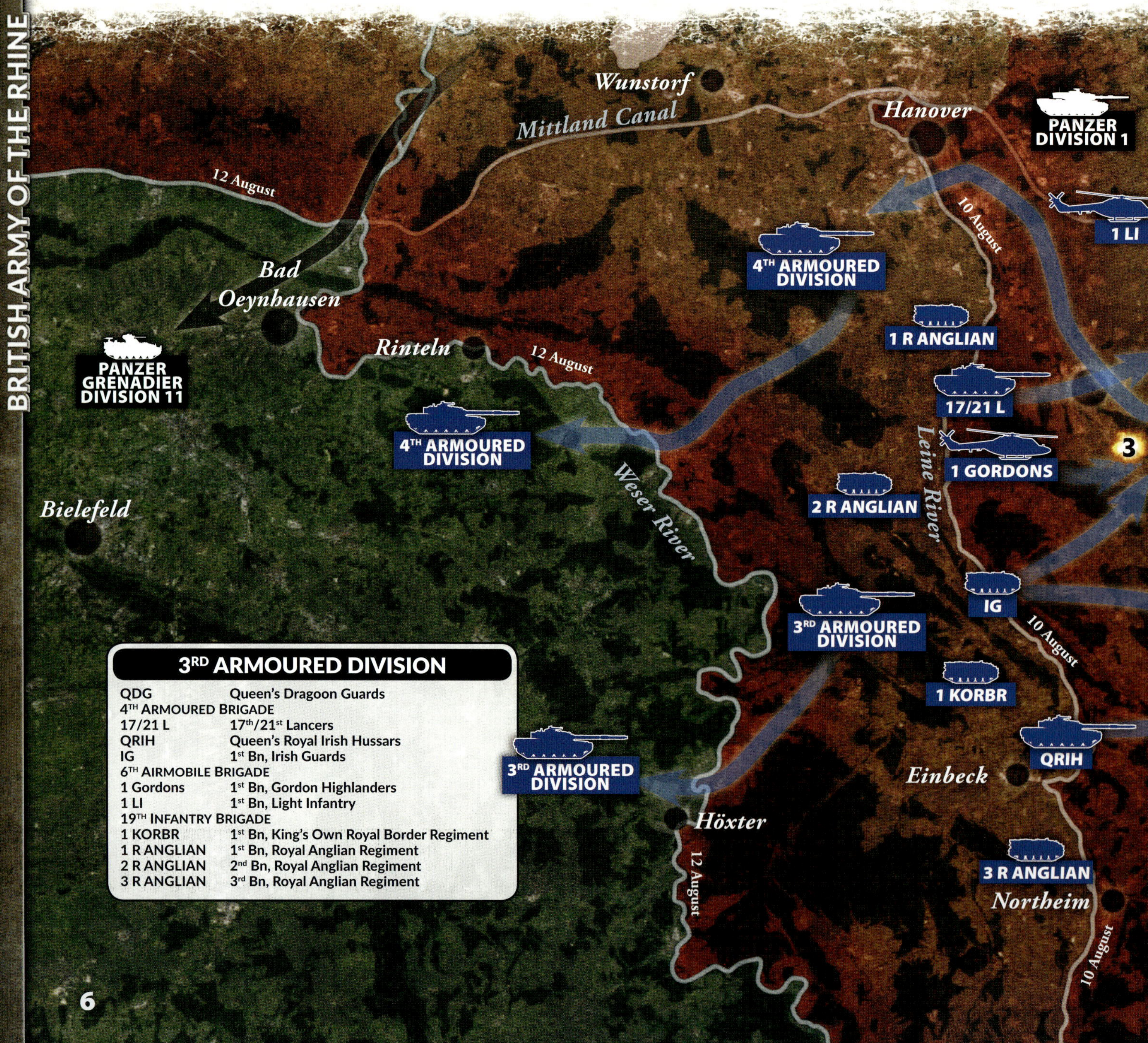

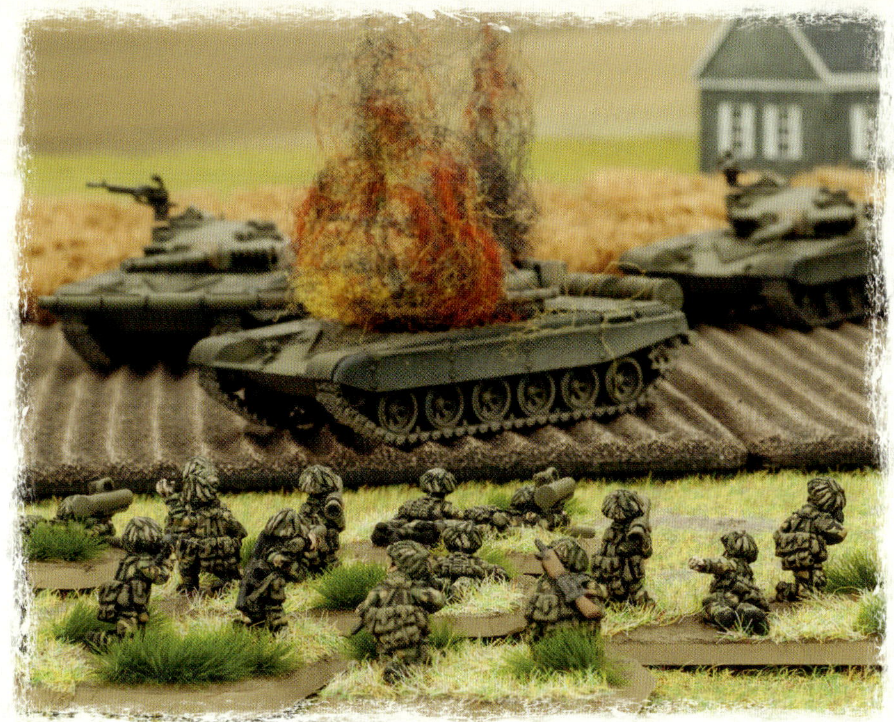

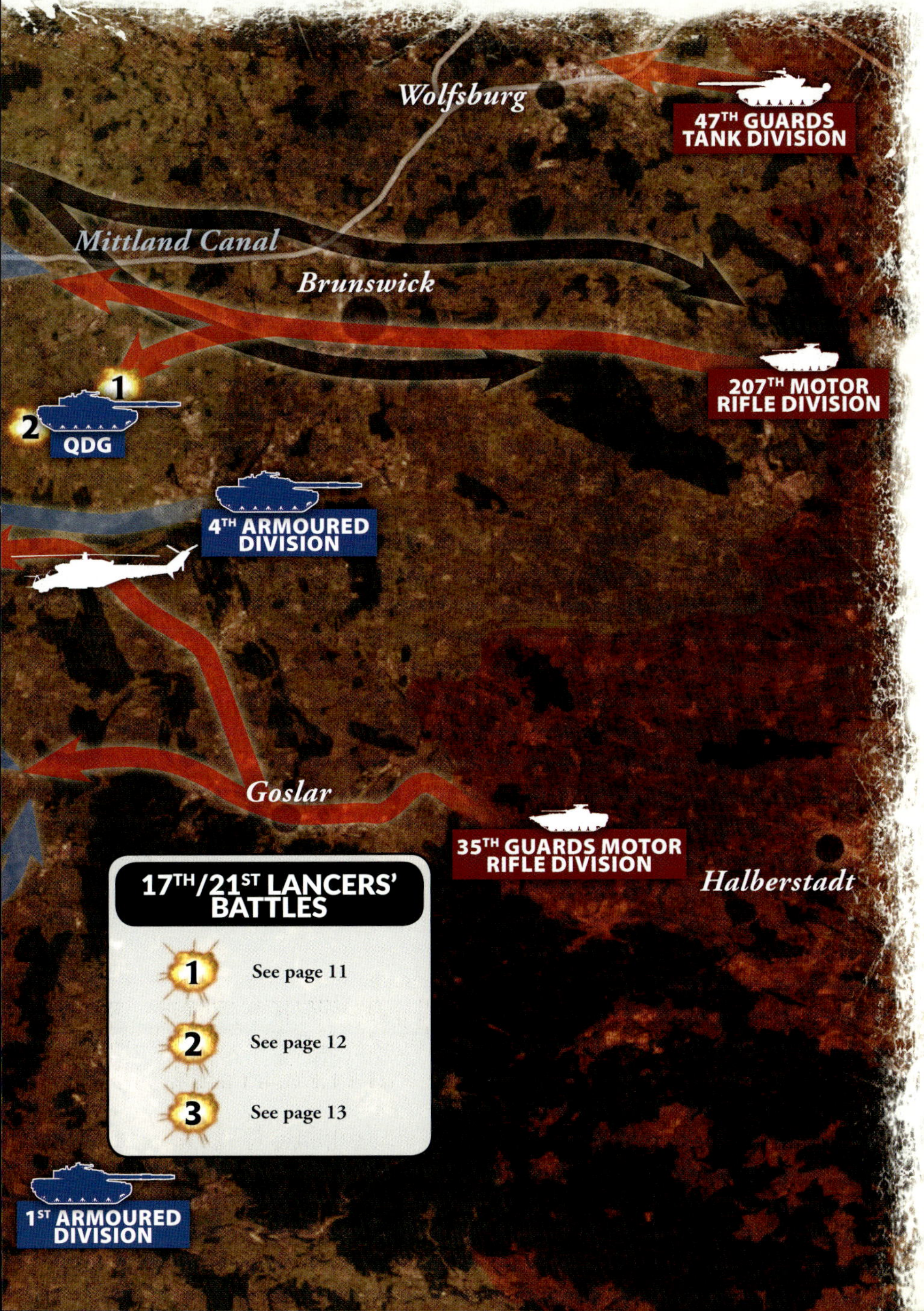

17TH/21ST LANCERS' BATTLES

1 See page 11

2 See page 12

3 See page 13

With the battered 4th Armoured Division safely behind the Leine River, the 3rd Armoured Division held the line as far south as Northeim where it linked into the defences of the 1st Armoured Division. There they rebuffed several attempts by the leading Soviet regiments to gain a foothold over the river.

With the Germans withdrawing in the north after a failed counterattack, the British attempt to hold a defensive line on the Leine River running south from Hannover was doomed to failure. The 4th Armoured Division now stretched back on the left flank, linking up with I German Corps which was taking up positions nearly at right angles to the British front along the Mittland Canal, and unless the 3rd Armoured Division conformed with this movement, it stood to be outflanked.

On the night of 11 August, in a lull as the Soviet forces regrouped for a major effort to cross the Leine, 3rd Armoured Division thinned out its defences on the Leine and withdrew to the Weser River. When the Soviet attacks began at dawn, most of their massive artillery preparation fell on empty positions.

The 17th/21st Lancers, Queen's Royal Irish Hussars and the Irish Guards battlegroups, with their flanks covered by the Queen's Dragoon Guards hammered the Soviets as they crossed the Leine, then withdrew before the Soviets could make a concentrated response. Turning to fight every inch of the way, they made the advancing Soviet divisions pay a high price for their gains, reducing their 'dash to the Rhine' to a crawl.

Where the Soviet spearheads did manage to find gaps and outflank the British rearguard, they found the airmobile battalions of the Gordon Highlanders and the Light Infantry bristling with Milan anti-tank missiles blocking their way.

It was late in the night of 12 August that 4th Armoured Brigade made its way across the Wesser bridges, with the Scorpions and Scimitars of their recce troops dashing back across, just before the bridges were blown.

There would be no rest however. Leaving the infantry of 19th Brigade to hold the Weser River, 4th Armoured Brigade faced north to support the 4th Armoured Division as they joined in the major NATO counterattack towards Bremerhaven.

CALL SIGN CHARLIE

Major Charles Leslie was strolling back through the woods from checking on young Hawkes' 'Fighting Micks'. The Irish Guardsmen of his attached infantry platoon seemed cheery enough, and the sergeant had everything in hand. The platoon was dug in with their Milan anti-tank missiles covering the approaches, even in this temporary hide. It was a lovely summer's day and a good day to be in command of a squadron, especially of his squadron, C Squadron of the 17th/21st Lancers, the famed Death or Glory Boys.

He'd already visited Turner's and Spencer's troops and the three Chieftains of Lieutenant Brown's 12 Troop were in the tree line ahead. 'Lovely beasties,' he thought. 'Best bloody tank out there.' With the new Stillbrew package, they were damn near invulnerable from the front and the 120mm gun packed a wallop that would turn any Russian tank inside out.

Leslie's reverie was shattered by the howl of a pair of Russian jets screaming in at low level, the roar of their cannon ripping through the stillness. Looking up from the ground, part of him noticed that he didn't remember dropping prone, while the rest watched with fascination as a Blowpipe missile streaked after the departing jets. Moments later the rearmost flicked to the left as the missile blew off a tailplane, reared up, then exploded.

Satisfying as it was to contemplate the abrupt end of the Russian menace, the column of smoke and shouting coming from the village of Klein Escherde had him jogging across the field in moments. The sight that greeted him was pandemonium. It looked like the Swingfire anti-tank missile carriers of the guided weapons troop were intact, but two trucks were burning and at least two squaddies and three civilians were framed by clusters of concerned soldiers and locals. Sergeant Mathie detached himself and walked over as Leslie approached.

'Smitty'll be OK, but Nobby's dead sir.' The sergeant looked stunned by the suddenness of the tragedy.

The day seemed suddenly colder. Leslie shivered and looked up, surprised to see the sun still shining brightly in a cloudless sky.

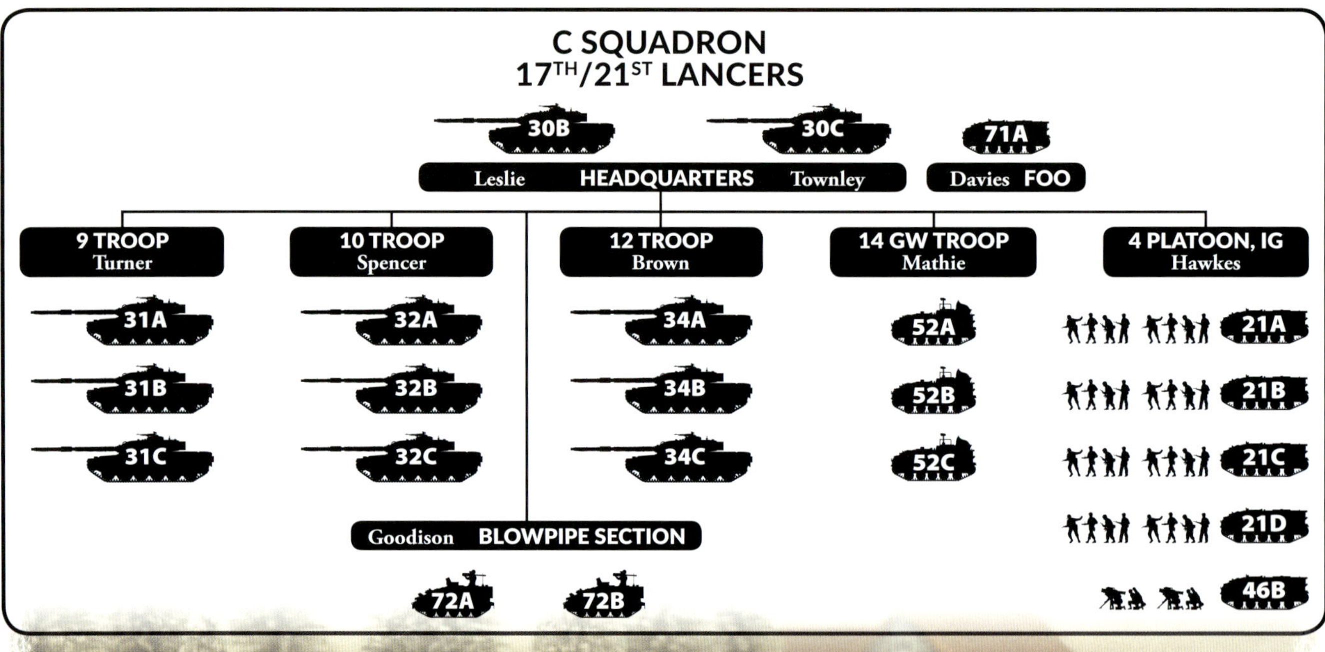

THE BREAKTHROUGH (map on page 12)

11:15 hours, Wednesday 7 August

The Welsh Cavalry, as the Queen's Dragoon Guards were known, received the expected signal. After three days of intense fighting, and heavy losses, a Soviet battlegroup had broken through the 4th Armoured Division and was racing for the Leine River crossings. The regiment's job would be to work out where they were going, then delay them to buy time for the Death or Glory Boys' Battlegroup to get ready to stop them.

It was A Squadron, reinforced by Lieutenant (pronounced 'lef-tenant' in the British Army) Brown's troop of Chieftain tanks, that found the Soviet spearhead near the village of Steinbrück racing down the highway from Brunswick. The Welsh Cavalry's Scorpion and Scimitar light tanks quickly dealt with the leading BMP scout vehicles as they crossed the stream, but were no match for the company of heavier T-72 tanks that followed. That's when their Striker guided-weapons troop with their Swingfire missiles entered the fray. Backed by the Chieftain tanks with their supremely powerful 120mm guns, they managed to halt the Soviet forward detachment, although the Queens Dragoon Guards lost a number of tanks and Brown's troop lost a Chieftain in the process.

Breaking free, the QDG Squadron raced back along the highway, passing through the Death or Glory Boy's lines at Schellerten as the sappers finished laying the last of their hasty minefields.

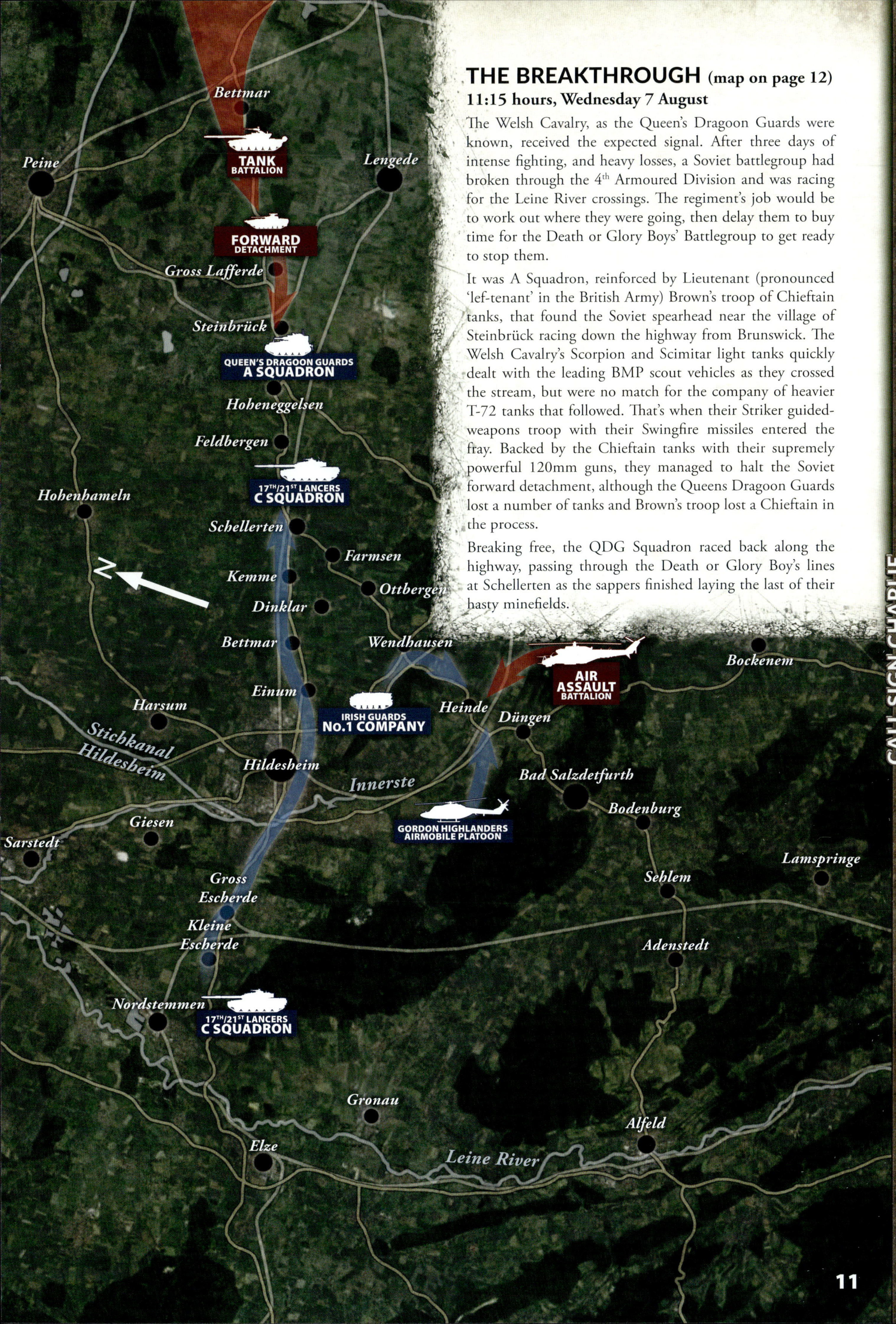

HOLD THE LINE

16:20 hours, Wednesday 7 August

The C Squadron team that reached Schellerten in the early morning of the fourth day of the war was little more than a skeleton. With two troops of tanks attached to the Welsh Cavalry (against the protests of Major Leslie) and a third with the Micks, swapped for their infantry platoon, all that was left was Spencer's troop of three tanks, two more in the Squadron HQ, the Swingfire troop, the Irish Guards infantry platoon, and the artillery observer with a troop of Abbots on call as artillery support.

Brown's troop arrived mid-afternoon with the retreating Welsh Cavalry, but needed fuel and ammunition before it would be fit to fight, so was sent to the rear of the town to bomb up.

Unfortunately the Soviet forward detachment arrived before any of the promised British reinforcements.

The remainder of the T-72 battalion that had run into the Queen's Dragoon Guards at Steinbrück attacked late

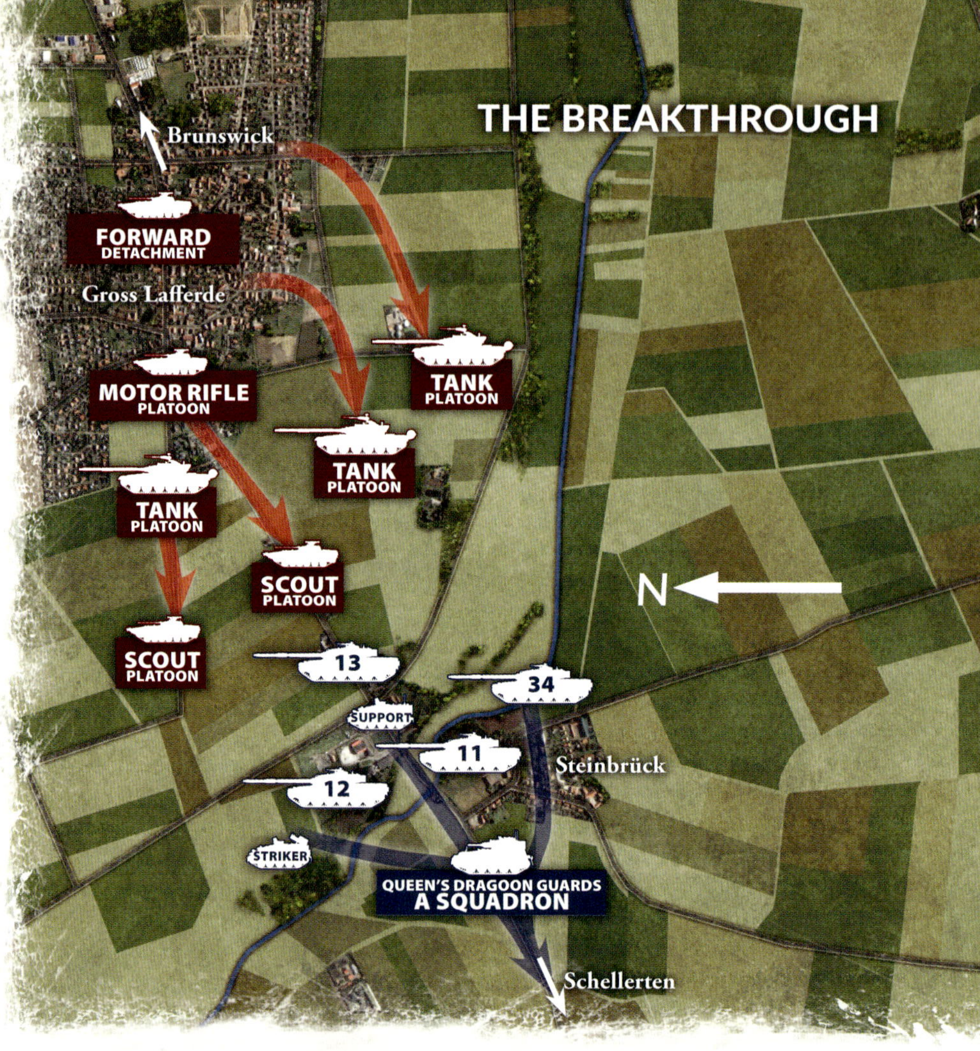

in the afternoon, backed by SU-25 Frogfoot strike aircraft, Mi-24 Hind attack helicopters and artillery. The Soviet infantry company pushed down the rail line, assaulting the factory on the outskirts of town under covering fire from their BMP fighting vehicles. Ably supported by the Royal Artillery, the Micks held despite heavy casualties, even resorting to a bayonet charge to regain positions overrun by the Soviet advance.

Meanwhile the T-72 tanks advanced at speed into the fire of the Chieftains and Swingfire missile carriers. After losing a tank, Spencer's troop fell back into the outskirts of Schellerten, losing another soon after to a helicopter's missile.

The timely arrival of Lieutenant Turner's 9 Troop and a flight of Lynx HELARM helicopters slowed the Soviet advance, while the Blowpipe section forced the Soviet Air Force to be more cautious in its attacks.

A renewed Soviet attack nearly overran the British position until a well-timed air strike by Harrier jump jets and a counterattack by Brown's two surviving tanks restored the situation.

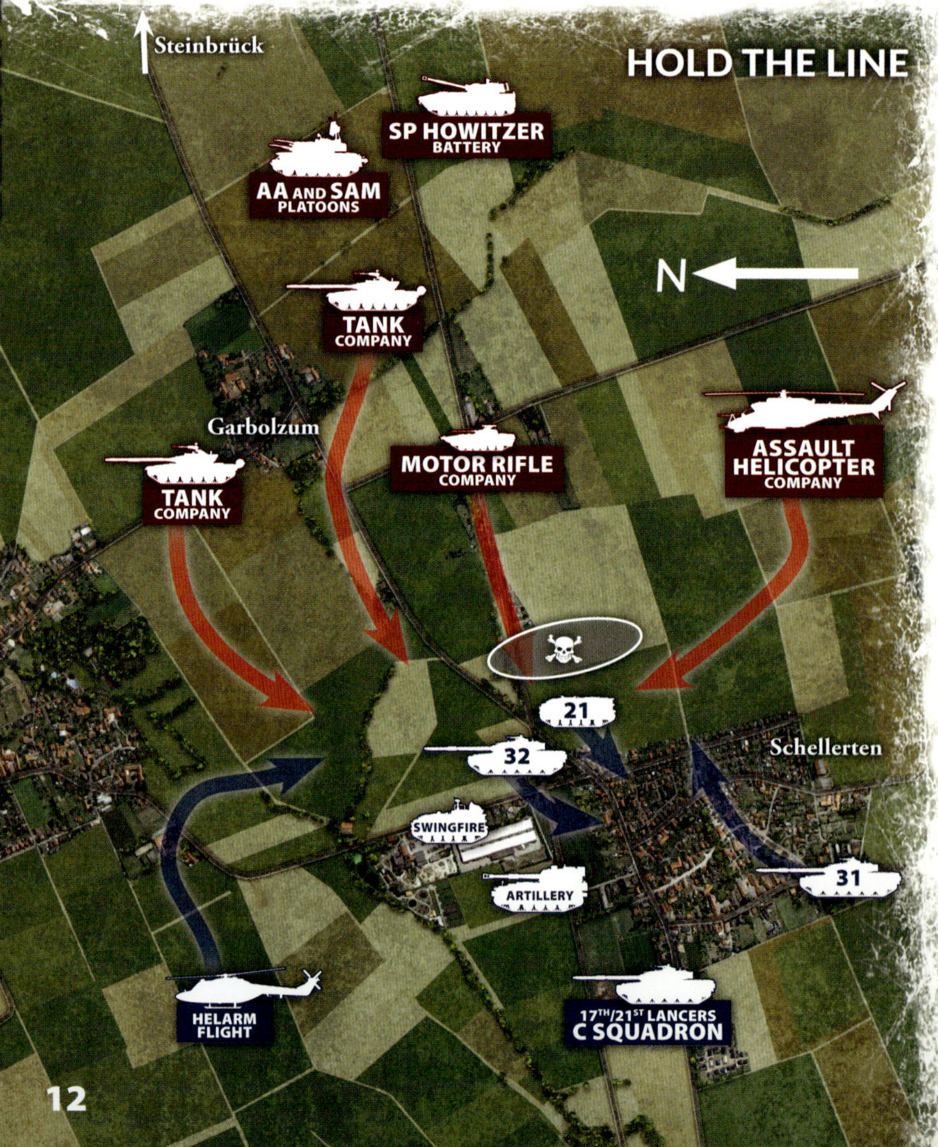

BRIDGE AT HEINDE
18:00 hours, Wednesday 7 August

While Major Leslie's C Squadron was fighting for its life at Schellerten, another, possibly more dangerous threat was developing behind them. The Innerste River ran across their line of retreat. If things went sour, the bridges at Heinde would be an essential escape route. If they went well, they would be equally essential for the 'loggies', the logistics boys, bringing up the fuel and ammunition they'd desperately need after a hard fight.

When an assault landing by a Soviet air assault battalion took the bridges at 18:00 hours, cutting off the British force, there was little available to retake them.

The only troops in the area were part of No. 1 Company of the Irish Guards who were hastily ordered to retake the bridge before continuing with their assigned task of establishing a blocking position to the east.

The Micks were making little headway under constant Soviet air attack until the Chieftains of 11 Troop turned up escorting a section of Tracked Rapier anti-aircraft missiles, just as an airmobile platoon from the 'Gay Gordons' landed on the far side of the bridge. Under cover of a heavy mortar barrage, the Micks and the Gordons finally retook the bridges at bayonet point in the dark of a cloudy night.

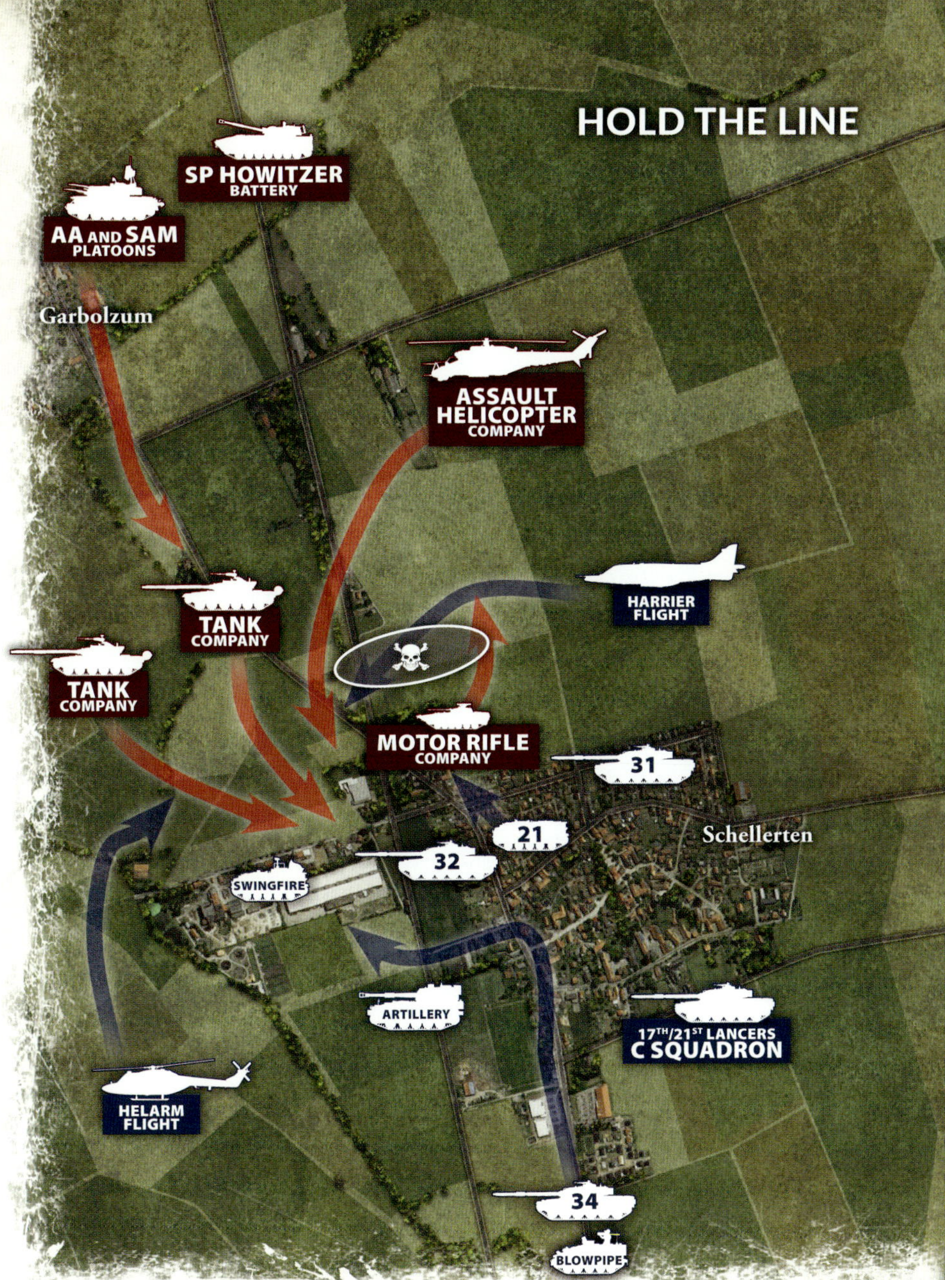

BRIDGE AT HEINDE

BACK TO THE LEINE
Afternoon, Saturday 10 August

C Squadron, battered and bruised, but still fighting, crossed the Leine River at Alfeld in the early afternoon of the seventh day of the war. Four days of continuous fighting, and a slow but steady retreat, had left the men exhausted and the tanks in desperate need of maintenance.

3rd Armoured Division had done its job. It had held the line long enough for the 1st and 4th Armoured Divisions to reform a defensive line on the Leine River. A few days' rest, if the Soviets didn't make another breakthrough, and they'd be back in the line again. Now though, all they wanted to do was sleep.

IRON DIVISION FORCES

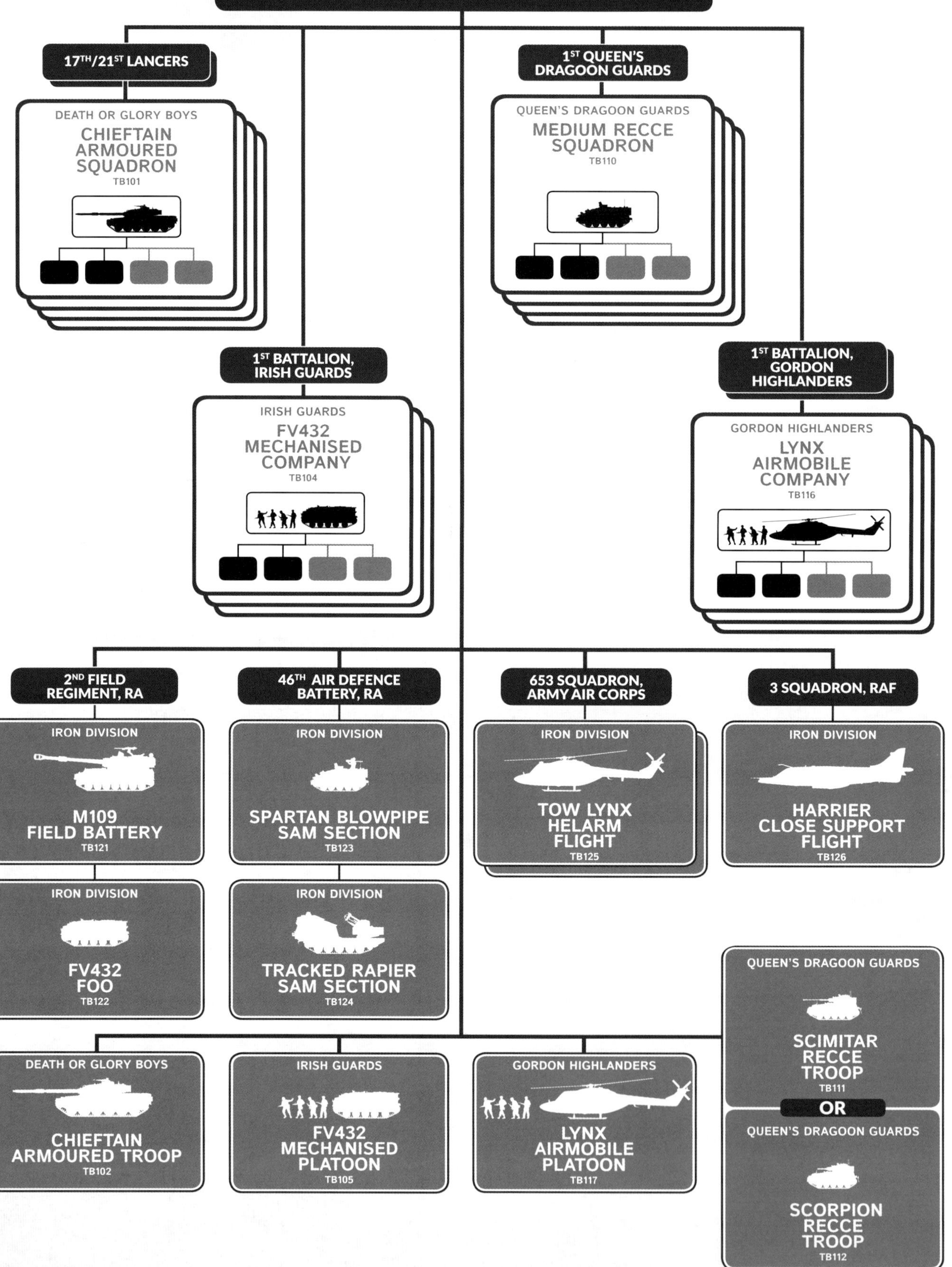

A silence fell over the Ops tent as the assembled commanders and staff officers waited for the General to finish the O Group as he always had during training exercises, by delivering a few well-chosen words of encouragement.

With a deliberateness, due as much from days of harried activity and near sleepless nights as from his usual calm steadiness, the General rose to his feet, made his way to the front of the assembled officers and turned his back on the map that displayed the division's battle plan. Standing before his brigade commanders, he couldn't help but appreciate that they represented more than the sum total of the men and machines they would soon be leading into battle.

Though he could not see them, the General knew behind each officer there were ranks upon ranks of ghosts belonging to the soldiers who had won the reputation his commanders were charged with upholding. Those ethereal spectres had followed Marlborough at Blenheim, clung to the stirrups of the Scots Greys as they rode down the French at Waterloo, checked the German onslaught at Mons, and bested the Desert Fox at El Alamein. In the coming fight he and his officers would carry more than the responsibilities their assigned duties required them to shoulder. They would be expected to add to the battle honours their predecessors had earned for their regiments with their blood.

With that in mind, he drew in a deep breath and, in a voice that betrayed neither fear nor trepidation, spoke. 'Gentlemen, we know what is expected of us. Now, let's be about our business.'

Like most British formations, the 3rd Armoured Division has a long and storied history, serving against Napoleon in the Peninsula and at the Battle of Waterloo, against the Russians in the Crimean War, once more in the Second Boer War, and then again in both World Wars, gaining the nickname 'Iron Division' for its fortitude and unwavering determination. Unusually for an armoured division, it has an armoured brigade, an infantry brigade, and Britain's only airmobile brigade, giving it a unique set of capabilities.

Knowing that it will have to stop Soviet armoured thrusts that outnumber it in tanks several times over, the division's plan is a layered defence to take the sting out of the Soviet punch, slow them down, then destroy them with massed firepower. The first to contact the enemy is the covering force made up of the light tanks of the 1st Queen's Dragoon Guards backed up by heavier forces as needed. Their job is to stop the Soviet reconnaissance elements from locating the British defences, forcing their tanks to assault blind into the teeth of the defences.

Once the Soviet thrust has been channelled into a planned killing zone, the heavyweights of the Death or Glory Boys take over. British doctrine calls for their tanks to be tough and capable of dishing out a lot of punishment, and the Chieftain fits this bill. It's not fast, but once in a prepared defensive position, it's deadly. That's why the covering force has such an important job making sure they know where the Soviet thrust is heading and have time to prepare for it.

The tanks are not well suited to fighting in woods and villages, so that's where the infantry of the Irish Guards come in. When supported by their Milan anti-tank missiles, they are excellent for holding a village. The Soviets cannot afford to bypass them, taking missile fire in the flank, but will spend a lot of time trying to dig them out, suffering casualties all the time. Meanwhile, the Chieftains are engaging them from the front, and the Soviet advance is suffering heavily for every metre gained.

If all of this fails, or the Soviets manage to elude the reconnaissance element, the airmobile infantry of the Gordon Highlanders step in, or more precisely fly in. The airmobile infantry have an extraordinary number of Milan anti-tank guided missiles and the mobility of their Lynx transport helicopters, allowing them to form an anti-tank barrier wherever needed.

Once the Soviet advance has been ground down, the Iron Division will counterattack to regain lost ground. Like their defence, this is a methodical process rather than a lightning thrust. Keeping one foot on the ground at all times, and plenty of firepower on tap, the they will roll up the Soviets step by step as they push them back out of West Germany.

DEATH OR GLORY BOYS

Like all British cavalry regiments, the 17th/21st Lancers have a long and glorious history. The regiment gained its 'Death or Glory' badge and motto in honour of General Wolfe who died at the Battle of Quebec that ended French rule in Canada. The 17th and 21st Lancers fought in the American War of Independence and against Napoleon and his allies in the Eighteenth Century, against the Russians (taking part in the famous Charge of the Light Brigade) and throughout India and Africa in the Nineteenth Century, and in both World Wars.

After serving on the Western Front in the First World War where their mobility allowed them to take a significant part in the battles of 1918, the 17th (Duke of Cambridge's Own) Lancers were amalgamated with the 21st (Empress of India's) Lancers to form the new 17th/21st Lancers.

The new regiment converted to tanks before the Second World War. There they fought in the key battles of the Tunisian and Italian Campaigns, earning new battle honours. Since then, the regiment has deployed all over the world including Greece, Palestine, Aden, and Hong Kong, and served stints in Northern Ireland and in the British Army Of the Rhine (BAOR).

The 17th/21st Lancers returned to Germany, joining the 4th Armoured Brigade, in 1981, before taking part in Operation Lionheart 1984, a major exercise to test the British Army's readiness. They performed well, and the increased familiarity with their assigned battle area paid dividends when the time came to fight for real.

The 'Death or Glory Boys' were ready when the time came and made the Soviets pay a high price for every inch of ground.

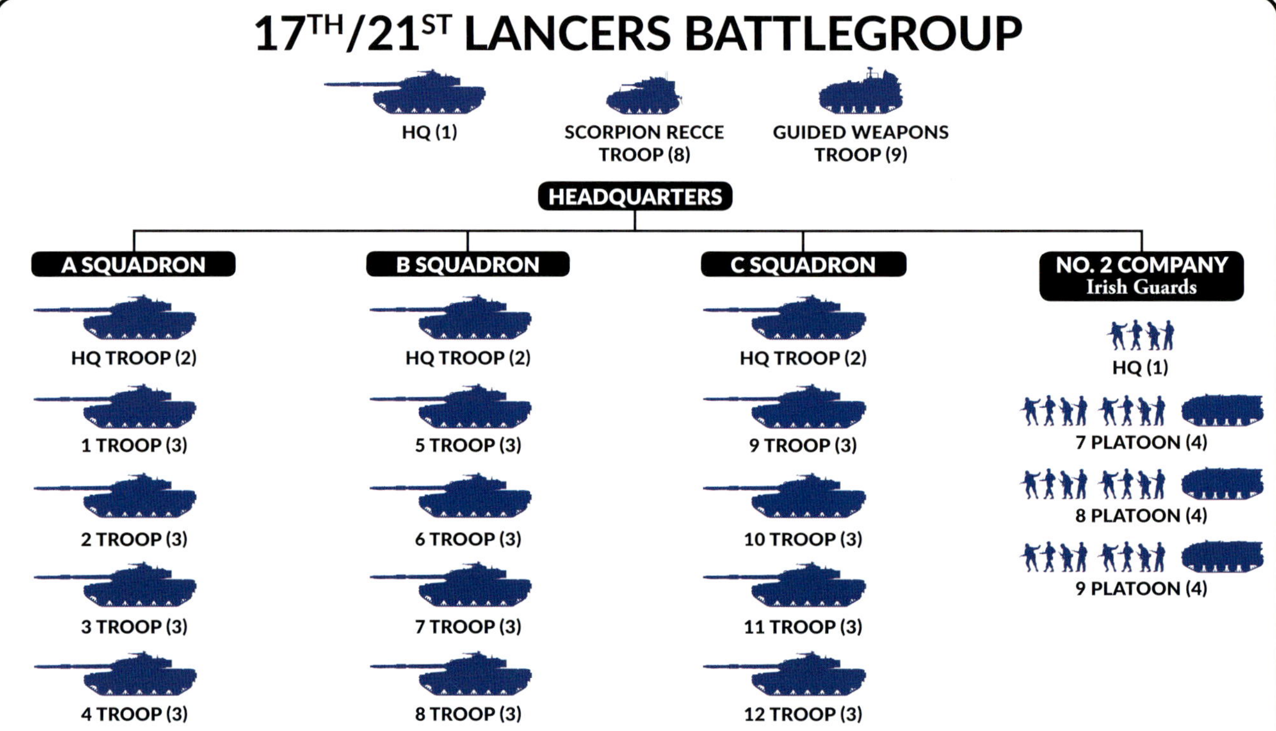

The British Army cross-attaches squadrons and companies between the infantry battalions and (battalion-strength) cavalry regiments in a brigade to form all-arms battlegroups. In the 4th Armoured Brigade, the 17th/21st Lancers lent their D Squadron to the Irish Guards and received their No. 2 Company in return.

CHIEFTAIN ARMOURED SQUADRON

DEATH OR GLORY BOYS

CHIEFTAIN ARMOURED SQUADRON HQ
TB101

| 2x Chieftain | **12 POINTS** |
| 1x Chieftain | **6 POINTS** |

OPTIONS

• Replace any or all Chieftain tanks with Chieftain Stillbrew for +1 point each.

Chieftain Stillbrew has Front armour 18 instead of 17, and Cross 3+ instead of 2+.

DEATH OR GLORY BOYS

CHIEFTAIN ARMOURED TROOP
TB102

DEATH OR GLORY BOYS

CHIEFTAIN ARMOURED TROOP
TB102

DEATH OR GLORY BOYS

SWINGFIRE GUIDED WEAPONS TROOP
TB103

QUEEN'S DRAGOON GUARDS

SCORPION RECCE TROOP
TB112

DEATH OR GLORY BOYS

CHIEFTAIN ARMOURED TROOP
TB102

DEATH OR GLORY BOYS

CHIEFTAIN ARMOURED TROOP
TB102

IRON DIVISION

ABBOT FIELD BATTERY
TB120

IRISH GUARDS

FV432 MECHANISED PLATOON
TB105

CHIEFTAIN ARMOURED TROOP

CHIEFTAIN ARMOURED TROOP

3x Chieftain	**18 POINTS**
2x Chieftain	**12 POINTS**

OPTIONS

- Replace any or all Chieftain tanks with Chieftain Stillbrew for +1 point each.

Chieftain Stillbrew has Front armour 18 instead of 17, and Cross 3+ instead of 2+.

• TANK UNIT • BAZOOKA SKIRTS • INFRA-RED (IR) •

COURAGE 4+	SKILL 3+
MORALE 4+	ASSAULT 3+
REMOUNT 3+	COUNTERATTACK 4+

IS HIT ON 4+

FRONT / STILLBREW	SIDE	TOP
17 / 18	6	2

TACTICAL	TERRAIN DASH	CROSS COUNTRY DASH	ROAD DASH	CROSS / STILLBREW
10"/25cm	14"/35cm	20"/50cm	24"/60cm	2+ / 3+

WEAPON	RANGE	ROF HALTED	ROF MOVING	ANTI-TANK	FIRE-POWER	NOTES
120mm L11 gun	40"/100cm	2	1	22	2+	Brutal, Laser Rangefinder, Smoke, Stabiliser
7.62mm AA MG	16"/40cm	3	3	2	6	
7.62mm MG	16"/40cm	1	1	2	6	

Crew:	*4 - commander, gunner, loader, driver*	*Weapons:*	*120mm L11 gun* *2x 7.62mm L7 MG*
Weight:	*56 tonnes*	*Armour:*	*195mm*
Length:	*10.77m (34' 4")*	*Speed:*	*48 km/h (30 mph)*
Width:	*3.66m (12')*	*Engine:*	*Leyland L60 horizontally opposed, multi-fuel engine 560 kW (750 hp)*
Height:	*2.99m (9'6")*		

The British fought the Second World War in fast light tanks, outgunned by their opponents. Now, the Chieftain tank has the thickest armour and biggest gun of any tank in NATO.

When it entered service in 1966, the Chieftain was a behemoth capable of overpowering any tank in existence. It still is, despite twenty years of evolution in tank design, a tough opponent. This evolution has not passed the Chieftain by. The front of its turret now bears a layer of 'Stillbrew' armour, maintaining its edge as one of the best protected tanks in the world.

The massive rifled 120mm gun has also withstood the test of time. It uses a separate charge and round which allowed more ammunition to be carried, with less chance of the tank 'brewing up' when hit. Firing the latest anti-tank rounds, it can penetrate any tank in existence at long range, while its HESH (High Explosive Squash Head) rounds are extremely deadly against troops in buildings and bunkers.

The lone Scorpion raced through its troop's position as if the devil himself was after it, 2nd Lieutenant Martin Spencer wondered what it was about. Odds and sods of the Welsh Cavalry had been going back and forth all day, though during the last hour they'd mostly been going. The young troop commander wondered if he'd somehow missed something, like word the covering force battle was over and it was nearing the time when he would see if his trio of Chieftains were as good as his instructors back at Bovington had claimed they were.

Spencer watched the Scorpion until it had disappeared into the thick forest that concealed the tanks of A Squadron, 17th/21st Lancers. Odd, he thought, that something like the cavalry's passage of lines should take place without his OC notifying him of it. Spencer was still mulling over this disquieting thought when he caught sight of another vehicle nosing down the same road the Scorpion had come barrelling down.

'Shit!' Without thinking he flicked the selector on his chest harness to the squadron net. 'Charlie Charlie Three Two, this is Three Two Alpha, Contact, Contact, T72s to your front, engage, out.' A second flick as Martin selected the crew intercom. 'Target, Right, On, T72 in open, Fin, On!'

'Fin, Lasing…, On.' Trooper McReadie replied without a hint of his normal stutter, his eyes glued to the rubber of his optic. Martin glanced left at his loader to check before his next command. 'Loaded, fire!'

'Firing now… Target.' For a moment Martin paused as he wondered why his Scouse trooper's stutter had vanished before pulling himself back to the job in hand. 'Target. Nice shot Mac. Next target right, BMP-2 ducking into the wood line, On, Fin, On!'

'Firing now… Target.'

'Target, stop. Driver reverse and move to secondary.' Another flick to the squadron net. 'Hello Charlie Charlie Three Two, this is Three Two Alpha. Disengage and move to secondary positions, out to you. Hello Zero Alpha this is Three Two Alpha, Contact NOW. Grid Whiskey Mike 274165. Looks like a Combat Recce Patrol. Moving to….SHIT!'

In the Squadron CP no one said a word as the young officer's transmission ended abruptly.

DEATH OR GLORY BOYS

SWINGFIRE GUIDED WEAPONS TROOP

SWINGFIRE GUIDED WEAPONS TROOP	
3x Swingfire	**6 POINTS**
2x Swingfire	**4 POINTS**

The Swingfire missile is somewhat unique in two respects. Firstly, it can 'swing' up to 90 degrees on launch, giving it a very wide field of fire. Secondly, the gunner can remotely control the missile launcher from up to 50m (165 feet) away. This allows the FV438 Swingfire launch vehicle to be positioned in cover, or even out of sight of the enemy when it fires.

Like many things British, the Swingfire is a little old fashioned. It is a huge missile with a long range and an exceptionally powerful warhead, but it takes a while to bring under the operator's control. Deploy your Swingfires behind your combat troops, using their long range to protect them from unwanted attention.

• TANK UNIT • SWINGFIRE • THERMAL IMAGING •

COURAGE 4+	SKILL 3+
MORALE 4+	ASSAULT 4+
REMOUNT 4+	COUNTERATTACK 5+

IS HIT ON 4+		
FRONT	SIDE	TOP
1	1	1

TACTICAL	TERRAIN DASH	CROSS COUNTRY DASH	ROAD DASH	CROSS
10"/25cm	14"/35cm	20"/50cm	24"/60cm	3+

WEAPON	RANGE	ROF HALTED	ROF MOVING	ANTI-TANK	FIRE-POWER	NOTES
Swingfire missile	8"/20cm– 48"/120cm	1	-	23	3+	Guided, HEAT
7.62mm AA MG	16"/40cm	3	3	2	6	

Crew: 3 - commander, gunner, driver
Weight: 16 tonnes
Length: 5.10m (16'9")
Width: 3.00m (9'9")
Height: 2.70m (8'10")

Weapons: Swingfire guided missiles 1x 7.62mm L4 MG
Armour: 13mm
Speed: 52 km/h (33 mph)
Engine: Rolls-Royce K60 multi-fuel engine, 180 kW (240 hp)

IRISH GUARDS

The Irish Guards are one of the newest infantry regiments in the British Army, being formed in 1900. Despite this, as can be seen from its battle honours, 'The Micks' fought in almost every battle of both World Wars, fielding three battalions in each case. Unusually for a unit of Foot Guards, the 2nd Battalion fought in Sherman tanks as part of the Guards Armoured Division in North-West Europe in the later part of the war. The regiment won six Victoria Crosses, Britain's highest award for gallantry, in these wars.

After the war the regiment was once again reduced to a single battalion. Since then, it has served in Palestine, the Suez Canal Zone, Cyprus, Aden, Hong Kong, and Belize in Central America, along with regular stints as part of the British Army Of the Rhine. The one place the Irish Guards have not served is Northern Ireland, although they have suffered casualties from Irish Republican Army terrorist attacks.

In 1982, now a mechanised infantry battalion mounted in FV432 armoured personnel carriers, the Irish Guards rejoined the 4th Armoured Brigade in Germany, a post they had held in the mid 1970s before being sent to Belize.

As the only mechanised infantry battalion in the 3rd Armoured Division (the 1st and 4th Armoured Divisions both have four), the Irish Guards play a critical part in the division's war plans. To make the most use of their infantry, the Irish Guards often trade one of their companies to each armoured regiment, receiving an armoured squadron in return. This arrangement proved to work extremely well during the initial phases of the Soviet assault, and is likely to remain in use.

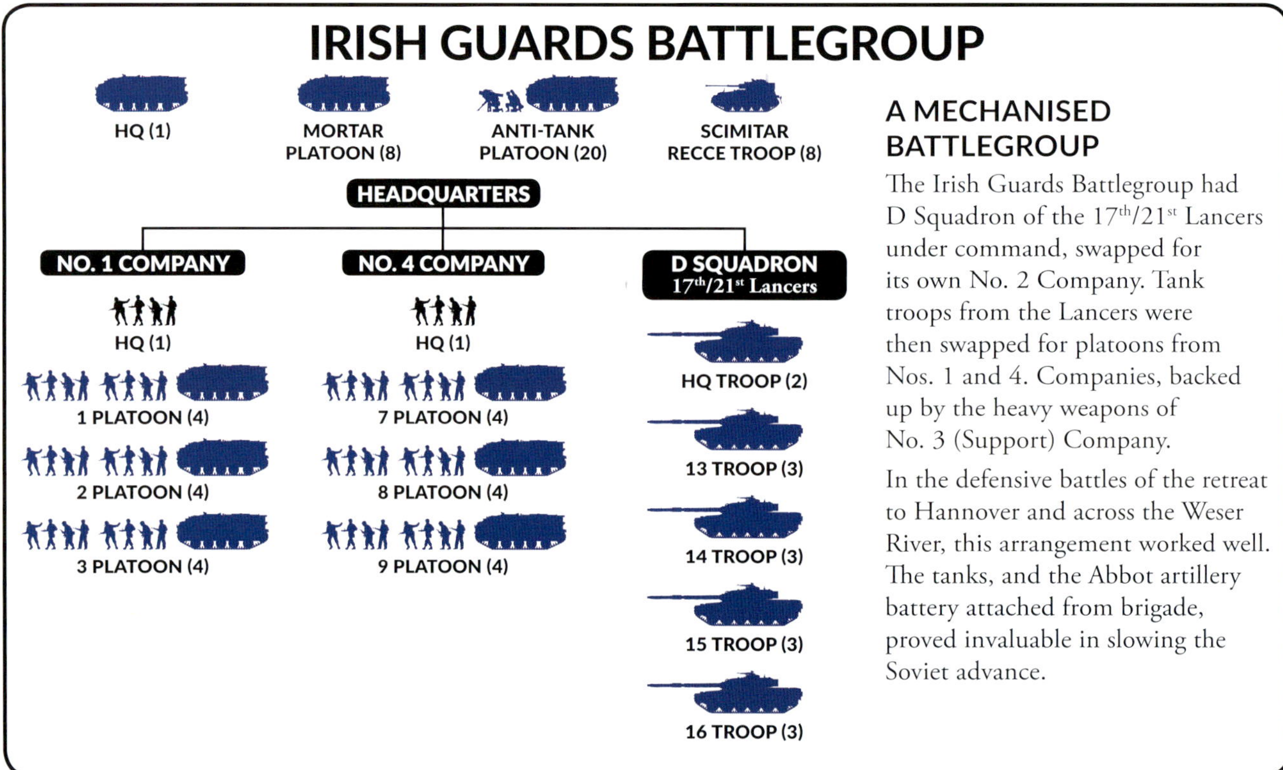

A MECHANISED BATTLEGROUP

The Irish Guards Battlegroup had D Squadron of the 17th/21st Lancers under command, swapped for its own No. 2 Company. Tank troops from the Lancers were then swapped for platoons from Nos. 1 and 4. Companies, backed up by the heavy weapons of No. 3 (Support) Company.

In the defensive battles of the retreat to Hannover and across the Weser River, this arrangement worked well. The tanks, and the Abbot artillery battery attached from brigade, proved invaluable in slowing the Soviet advance.

FV432 MECHANISED COMPANY

IRISH GUARDS

FV432 MECHANISED COMPANY HQ
TU104

1x SLR rifle team
1x FV432 [TB106]

1 POINT

OPTIONS
• Add up to two GPMG SF teams for +1 point each.
Each SF GPMG team must be attached to a FV432 Mechanised Platoon [TB106] before the game.

• INFANTRY FORMATION • HQ TRANSPORT •

COURAGE 3+	SKILL 2+
MORALE 3+	ASSAULT 3+
RALLY 3+	COUNTERATTACK 2+

IS HIT ON	INFANTRY SAVE
4+	3+

TACTICAL	TERRAIN DASH	CROSS COUNTRY DASH	ROAD DASH	CROSS
8"/20CM	8"/20CM	12"/30CM	12"/30CM	AUTO

WEAPON	RANGE	ROF HALTED	ROF MOVING	ANTI-TANK	FIRE-POWER	NOTES
SLR rifle team	16"/40CM	1	1	2	6	
SF GPMG team	24"/60CM	6	2	2	6	*Assault 4, Heavy Weapon*
or Artillery	40"/100CM	ARTILLERY		1	6	

IRISH GUARDS

FV432 MECHANISED PLATOON
TB106

IRISH GUARDS

FV432 MECHANISED PLATOON
TB106

IRISH GUARDS
FV432 MORTAR PLATOON
TB108

IRISH GUARDS
SPARTAN MOBILE MILAN SECTION
TB110

IRISH GUARDS

FV432 MECHANISED PLATOON
TB106

IRISH GUARDS

FV432 MILAN SECTION
TB109

QUEEN'S DRAGOON GUARDS
SCIMITAR RECCE TROOP
TB113

IRON DIVISION

ABBOT FIELD BATTERY
TB122

DEATH OR GLORY BOYS
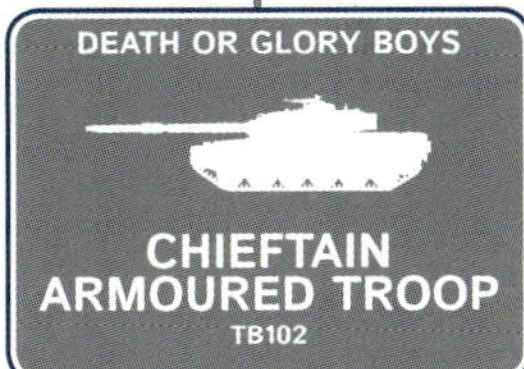
CHIEFTAIN ARMOURED TROOP
TB102

Second Lieutenant Peter Hawkes was near bricking himself in the dark crew compartment of his 432 as it rolled forward with an awful relentlessness. Fourteen months ago he'd been the scrawny fly half for the Rugby Second Fifteen at Ampleforth College, doing his damnedest to avoid getting caught up in the scrum. Now he was deliberately leading his platoon into the middle of a bloody nightmare.

When he'd signed up with the Irish Guards, it had been for three years guarding Buck House, the Tower and Windsor Castle. The worst, if luck was against him, would have been six months spent patrolling round Belfast or Londonderry. The very thought of debussing and storming an enemy position caused him to squeeze his hands tight around the fore grip of his SLR until his knuckles showed white.

His platoon sergeant, an apparently sleepy Ulsterman, reached over and grasped his hand with a fatherly touch. 'It'll be alright there sir. You'll do fine,' he advised with his typical gentle slowness. 'The lads know what to do.' Even as he spoke the APC braked viciously.

'Dismount! Dismount! Dismount!'

Peter emerged blinking like a barn owl as the sunlight all but blinded him. Only his drills kept him moving, peeling to the right and around to the front of the wagon where one and three sections were establishing the start line while two section hung back in reserve fifty meters to the rear. In front of him the smoke barrage from a battery of Abbots obscured the woodline that was his objective. Deciding he was as ready as he ever would be, he clicked the button on his radio. 'All Two One call signs, this is Two One Alpha, advance.' Then he commended his soul to God and stepped off.

FV432 MECHANISED PLATOON

FV432 MECHANISED PLATOON

4x GPMG team with 66mm anti-tank
3x Carl Gustav anti-tank team
1x 2" mortar team
4x FV432 [TB106]

7 POINTS

3x GPMG team with 66mm anti-tank
2x Carl Gustav anti-tank team
1x 2" mortar team
3x FV432 [TB106]

5 POINTS

OPTIONS
- Add two Milan missile teams & one FV432 [TB106] for +2 points.

• INFANTRY UNIT • INFRA-RED (IR) •

COURAGE 4+	SKILL 3+
MORALE 4+ RALLY 4+	ASSAULT 3+ COUNTERATTACK 3+

IS HIT ON	INFANTRY SAVE
4+	**3+**

TACTICAL	TERRAIN DASH	CROSS COUNTRY DASH	ROAD DASH	CROSS
8"/20CM	8"/20CM	12"/30CM	12"/30CM	AUTO

WEAPON	RANGE	ROF HALTED	ROF MOVING	ANTI-TANK	FIRE-POWER	NOTES
GPMG team	16"/40CM	3	2	2	6	
or 66mm anti-tank	12"/30CM	1	1	12	5+	HEAT, Slow Firing
Carl Gustav anti-tank team	16"/40CM	1	1	17	3+	HEAT, Slow Firing
2" mortar team	16"/40CM	1	1	2	4+	Assault 4, Overhead Fire, Slow Firing, Smoke
Milan missile	8"/20CM-36"/90CM	1	-	21	3+	Assault 4, Guided, HEAT

As the FV432 armoured personnel carrier was designed to carry a full section of infantry, the mechanised platoon mirrors the organisation of the standard rifle platoon with a HQ section and three rifle sections. The HQ section comprises a command group and a 2" light mortar team whose role is mainly to use smoke to blind enemy machine-guns.

The rifle sections break down into a machine-gun group armed with a 'Gimpy' (GPMG or General Purpose Machine-gun) and a number of L1A1 SLRs (Self-Loading Rifles) and a rifle group equipped with a 'Charlie G' (84mm Carl Gustav recoilless gun) for anti-tank work and more SLRs.

A tripod-mounted or support fire (SF) version of the GPMG is attached to platoons needing extra firepower or well sited for long-range harassing fire. Sections of two Milan anti-tank guided missiles are usually attached to platoons for additional anti-tank capability.

FV432 TRANSPORT

The FV432 armoured personnel carrier is the British equivalent of the ubiquitous American M113. The design is very conventional, being made of welded steel plates and capable of carrying a section of ten infantry.

The FV432 is used as a 'battle taxi', delivering the infantry to the battlefield safely protected from small arms and artillery fire. Once there, the infantry dismount to fight on foot, while the FV432 APCs retire behind cover, ready to provide a mobile reserve of fire in the event of an enemy infantry attack.

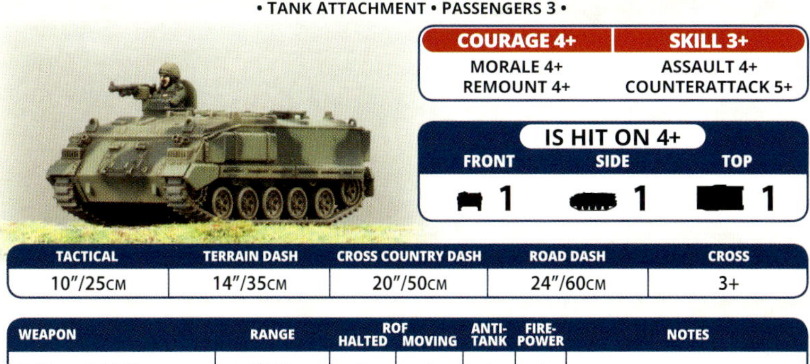

• TANK ATTACHMENT • PASSENGERS 3 •

COURAGE 4+	SKILL 3+
MORALE 4+ REMOUNT 4+	ASSAULT 4+ COUNTERATTACK 5+

IS HIT ON 4+		
FRONT	SIDE	TOP
1	1	1

TACTICAL	TERRAIN DASH	CROSS COUNTRY DASH	ROAD DASH	CROSS
10"/25CM	14"/35CM	20"/50CM	24"/60CM	3+

WEAPON	RANGE	ROF HALTED	ROF MOVING	ANTI-TANK	FIRE-POWER	NOTES
7.62mm AA MG	16"/40CM	3	3	2	6	

Crew:	2 – commander, driver	Weapons:	7.62mm L7 MG
Weight:	15 tonnes	Armour:	13mm
Length:	5.25m (17'3")	Speed:	52 km/h (33 mph)
Width:	2.53m (8'4")	Engine:	Rolls-Royce K60 multi-fuel
Height:	2.29m (7'6")		engine, 180 kW (240 hp)

IRISH GUARDS
FV432 MILAN SECTION

FV432 MILAN SECTION
4x Milan missile team
2x FV432 [TB106] — **4 POINTS**

2x Milan missile team
1x FV432 [TB106] — **2 POINTS**

The Milan missile is a modern man-portable, light anti-tank missile. Its small size makes the missile team easy to dig in and conceal, yet it can penetrate most tanks. A Soviet tank commander needs to think twice before attacking infantry protected by a Milan section.

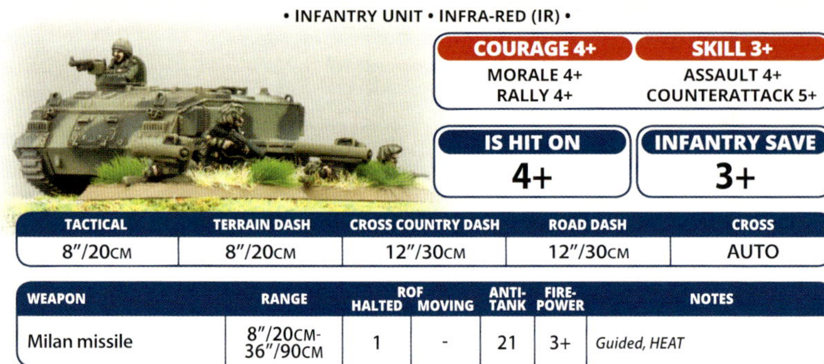

• INFANTRY UNIT • INFRA-RED (IR) •

COURAGE 4+	SKILL 3+
MORALE 4+	ASSAULT 4+
RALLY 4+	COUNTERATTACK 5+

IS HIT ON	INFANTRY SAVE
4+	3+

TACTICAL	TERRAIN DASH	CROSS COUNTRY DASH	ROAD DASH	CROSS
8"/20CM	8"/20CM	12"/30CM	12"/30CM	AUTO

WEAPON	RANGE	ROF HALTED	ROF MOVING	ANTI-TANK	FIRE-POWER	NOTES
Milan missile	8"/20CM-36"/90CM	1	-	21	3+	Guided, HEAT

IRISH GUARDS
SPARTAN MOBILE MILAN SECTION

SPARTAN MOBILE MILAN SECTION
4x Spartan MCT — **4 POINTS**

2x Spartan MCT — **2 POINTS**

As well as FV432-mounted Milan sections, the battalion anti-tank platoon has a mobile Milan section mounted in modified Spartan armoured personnel carriers. The mobile Milan section gives the infantry a useful anti-tank reserve with the speed to get where it is needed to bolster the unit's anti-tank defences.

The Spartan MCT (Milan Compact Turret) is based on Spartan, an armoured personnel carrier based on the light Scorpion reconnaissance tank chassis, mounting a small turret with a Milan missile launcher on each side.

• TANK UNIT • INFRA-RED (IR) •

COURAGE 4+	SKILL 3+
MORALE 4+	ASSAULT 4+
REMOUNT 4+	COUNTERATTACK 5+

IS HIT ON 4+		
FRONT	SIDE	TOP
2	1	1

TACTICAL	TERRAIN DASH	CROSS COUNTRY DASH	ROAD DASH	CROSS
10"/25CM	20"/50CM	28"/70CM	36"/90CM	3+

WEAPON	RANGE	ROF HALTED	ROF MOVING	ANTI-TANK	FIRE-POWER	NOTES
Milan missile	8"/20CM-36"/90CM	1	-	21	3+	Guided, HEAT
7.62mm AA MG	16"/40CM	3	3	2	6	

Crew:	3 - commander, gunner, driver	Weapons:	Milan guided missile
Weight:	8.5 tonnes		7.62mm L7 MG
Length:	4.93m (16'2")	Armour:	25mm Aluminium
Width:	2.24m (7'4")	Speed:	80 km/h (50 mph)
Height:	2.26m (7'5")	Engine:	Jaguar J60, 140 kW (190 hp)

FV432 MORTAR PLATOON

FV432 MORTAR PLATOON

8x FV432 mortar carrier	**4 POINTS**	
4x FV432 mortar carrier	**2 POINTS**	
2x FV432 mortar carrier	**1 POINTS**	

The mortar platoon mounts the reliable 81mm mortar in its FV432 APCs. The L16 mortar has excellent range and is very useful. With 160 mortar bombs, it can lay down quick bombardments to pin down enemy infantry, as well as firing sustained smoke bombardments to cover its own infantry in the assault.

• TANK UNIT •

COURAGE 4+	SKILL 3+
MORALE 4+	ASSAULT -
REMOUNT 4+	COUNTERATTACK -

IS HIT ON 4+

FRONT	SIDE	TOP
1	1	0

TACTICAL	TERRAIN DASH	CROSS COUNTRY DASH	ROAD DASH	CROSS
10"/25CM	14"/35CM	20"/50CM	24"/60CM	3+

WEAPON	RANGE	ROF HALTED	ROF MOVING	ANTI-TANK	FIRE-POWER	NOTES
81mm L16 mortar	56"/140CM	ARTILLERY		1	4+	*Smoke Bombardment*
7.62mm AA MG	16"/40CM	3	3	2	6	

GORDON HIGHLANDERS

The Gordon Highlanders were raised for the service in the Napoleonic Wars, fighting in India, the Netherlands, Egypt, Denmark, and Sicily, as well as in the Peninsula and at Waterloo with the Duke of Wellington. With Napoleon defeated, the Gordon Highlanders continued to fight in far flung corners of the globe for the rest of the 19th Century.

Recruiting mainly from Aberdeenshire in Scotland, the Gordons raised twenty two battalions for the First World War, an achievement reflected in their participation in every major battle on the Western Front, and even a few in Italy. After a disastrous start to the Second World War, losing two battalions trapped at St Valery-en-Caux with the 51st Highland Division, the Gordon Highlanders went on to fight in the British victories in North Africa, Italy, and North-West Europe.

The 1st Battalion, The Gordon Highlanders carries on this fine tradition as half of the 6th Airmobile Brigade. This experimental helicopter-mobile force is equipped with large numbers of MILAN anti-tank guided missiles, making it an ideal blocking force to stop unexpected Soviet thrusts.

Flown out from Britain at the start of hostilities, the Gordon Highlanders remained in reserve for the first few days as the armoured brigades were successfully slowing the Soviet advance in the British sector. This changed dramatically as the Dutch and West German Corps were forced back exposing the British flank.

The Gordon Highlanders soon found themselves stretched almost to breaking point as they parried repeated Soviet thrusts to cover the withdrawal to the Weser Line. Each time a company would be inserted along the Soviet thrust line. After breaking the Soviet momentum, but before the Soviet Army could mass to overwhelm them, they would break contact, remount their helicopters and leapfrog back to their next stop line.

LYNX AIRMOBILE COMPANY

• INFANTRY FORMATION •

GORDON HIGHLANDERS

LYNX AIRMOBILE COMPANY HQ
TB116

1x SLR rifle team	**1 POINT**

OPTIONS

• Add up to two GPMG SF teams for +1 point each.

Each SF GPMG team must be attached to a Lynx Airmobile Platoon [TB117] or Lynx Milan Platoon [TB118] before the game.

COURAGE 3+	**SKILL 2+**
MORALE 3+	ASSAULT 3+
RALLY 3+	COUNTERATTACK 2+

IS HIT ON	**INFANTRY SAVE**
4+	3+

TACTICAL	TERRAIN DASH	CROSS COUNTRY DASH	ROAD DASH	CROSS
8"/20cm	8"/20cm	12"/30cm	12"/30cm	AUTO

WEAPON	RANGE	ROF HALTED	ROF MOVING	ANTI-TANK	FIRE-POWER	NOTES
SLR rifle team	16"/40cm	1	1	2	6	
SF GPMG team	24"/60cm	6	2	2	6	*Assault 4, Heavy Weapon*
or Artillery	40"/100cm	ARTILLERY		1	6	

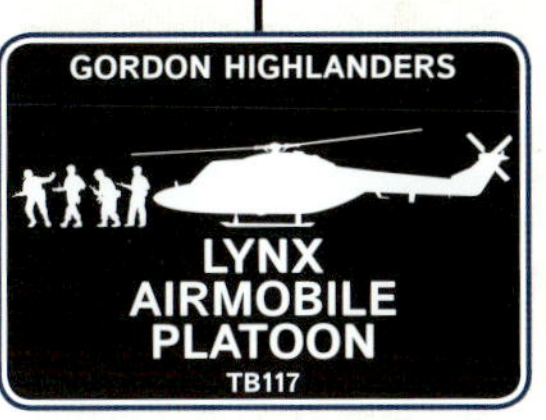

GORDON HIGHLANDERS

LYNX AIRMOBILE PLATOON
TB117

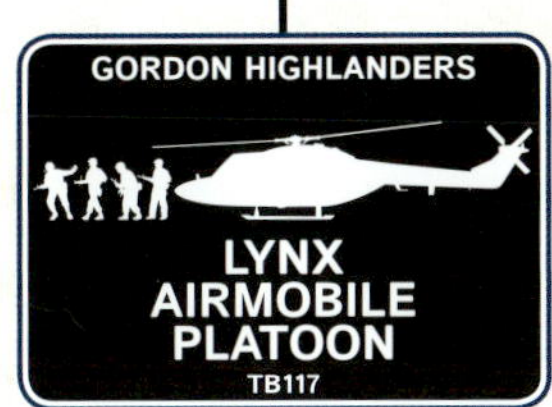

GORDON HIGHLANDERS

LYNX AIRMOBILE PLATOON
TB117

GORDON HIGHLANDERS

LYNX MILAN PLATOON
TB118

LYNX AIRMOBILE PLATOON

LYNX AIRMOBILE PLATOON

4x GPMG team with 66mm anti-tank
3x Milan missile team
1x 2" mortar team
3x Lynx [TB119]
7 POINTS

3x GPMG team with 66mm anti-tank
2x Milan missile team
1x 2" mortar team
2x Lynx [TB119]
5 POINTS

The 6th Armoured Brigade was re-rolled as the 6th Airmobile Brigade for Operation Lionheart 84 to test new concepts in airmobile anti-tank operations. Under the new structure, the 1st Gordon Highlanders and their sister regiment, the 2nd Light Infantry, were reorganised to have a much higher allocation of Milan anti-tank guided missiles and had their other equipment lightened to make them easily transported by helicopters.

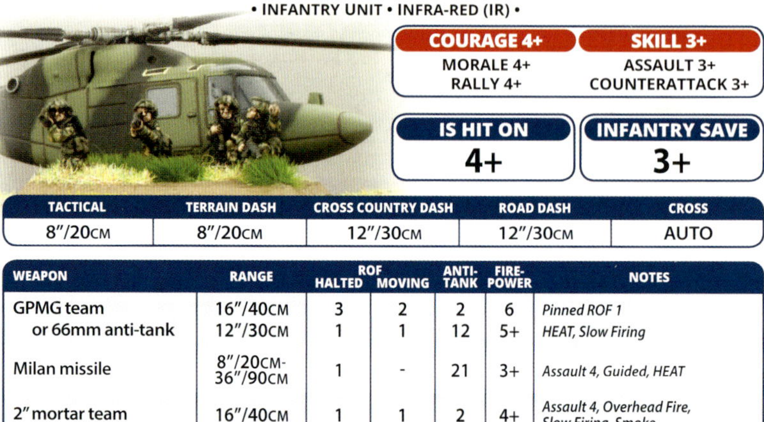

• INFANTRY UNIT • INFRA-RED (IR) •

COURAGE 4+	SKILL 3+
MORALE 4+	ASSAULT 3+
RALLY 4+	COUNTERATTACK 3+

IS HIT ON	INFANTRY SAVE
4+	3+

TACTICAL	TERRAIN DASH	CROSS COUNTRY DASH	ROAD DASH	CROSS
8"/20CM	8"/20CM	12"/30CM	12"/30CM	AUTO

WEAPON	RANGE	ROF HALTED	ROF MOVING	ANTI-TANK	FIRE-POWER	NOTES
GPMG team	16"/40CM	3	2	2	6	Pinned ROF 1
or 66mm anti-tank	12"/30CM	1	1	12	5+	HEAT, Slow Firing
Milan missile	8"/20CM-36"/90CM	1	-	21	3+	Assault 4, Guided, HEAT
2" mortar team	16"/40CM	1	1	2	4+	Assault 4, Overhead Fire, Slow Firing, Smoke

Their success during the exercise guaranteed the future of the concept, and with war looming, the number of Milan anti-tank missiles in the battalions was increased even further. Their final organisation had three Milan posts in each platoon, replacing the Carl Gustav recoilless anti-tank guns in a conventional rifle platoon. The GPMG was retained as the squad machine-gun to defend against infantry attacks.

LYNX MILAN PLATOON

LYNX MILAN PLATOON

8x Milan missile team
3x Lynx [TB119]
11 POINTS

6x Milan missile team
2x Lynx [TB119]
8 POINTS

4x MILAN missile team
2x Lynx [TB119]
5 POINTS

In line with the anti-tank role of the airmobile infantry, a third of the battalion's platoons are pure anti-tank units equipped with large numbers of Milan anti-tank guided missiles.

While vulnerable to dismounted infantry assault, these powerful anti-tank groups fulfil

• INFANTRY UNIT • INFRA-RED (IR) •

COURAGE 4+	SKILL 3+
MORALE 4+	ASSAULT 4+
RALLY 4+	COUNTERATTACK -

IS HIT ON	INFANTRY SAVE
4+	3+

TACTICAL	TERRAIN DASH	CROSS COUNTRY DASH	ROAD DASH	CROSS
8"/20CM	8"/20CM	12"/30CM	12"/30CM	AUTO

WEAPON	RANGE	HALTED	MOVING	ANTI-TANK	FIRE-POWER	NOTES
Milan missile	8"/20CM-36"/90CM	1	-	21	3+	Guided, HEAT

their role of breaking armoured assaults and slowing the Soviet advance. If the enemy resorts to a dismounted infantry attack, they have achieved their goal and break off, using their helicopters to reposition and prepare for the next tank attack.

LYNX TRANSPORT HELICOPTER

The Lynx is the British Army's new general purpose helicopter capable of carrying a fully-armed infantry section. Fast and fully aerobatic, the Lynx is ideal for the airmobile role as it can fly at tree-top level or lower to safely and quickly deliver its passengers to where they are needed.

As the airmobile infantry are neither expected nor equipped for insertion into 'hot' landing zones under fire, the Lynx is unarmed, lightening its load to enable it to carry plenty of extra missiles for its passengers.

TACTICAL	TERRAIN DASH	CROSS COUNTRY DASH	ROAD DASH	CROSS
UNLIMITED				AUTO

Crew:	2 – pilot, co-pilot	Armour:	None
Weight:	5.3 tonnes	Speed:	324 km/h (200 mph)
Length:	15.24m (50')	Engine:	Rolls-Royce Gem turboshaft,
Rotor:	12..80m (42')		835 kW (1,120 hp)

There wasn't a man in the Division who doubted that the troops Captain Charles Gordon commanded weren't tough little buggers. Gordon, known throughout the regiment as 'Bonnie Prince Charlie', took perverse pride in the ability of his men to give as good as they got in a punch up, particularly when it involved 'bluidy Sassenachs' as they called soldiers from the English regiments. But even the toughest of his lads had a limit, and he suspected they were fast approaching it.

They'd started the day just after dawn, when the company had been inserted on a piece of high ground just east of Bettmar from which they had ambushed the lead elements of a motorized rifle regiment. It was during their second hop that things began to go awry. Rather than setting down where Gordon had expected, a pair of Hinds on the prowl had caused the Lynx pilots to hastily dump the company two kilometres away. The overburdened GPMG and Milan teams had covered the distance in record time, hauling their cumbersome launchers and missiles to the tune of NCOs barking out encouragement and threats in equal measure. Still, they weren't quite quick enough. With no time to do a proper job, Gordon had no choice but to order his section commanders to find any piece of ground that offered some cover and prepare to fight. And though they'd managed to once more give as good as they got, it was a near run thing that had cost the company dearly.

Now, as the sun was finally giving way to the gathering darkness, his men were at the end of their tether. Then his CO ordered Gordon to check the Soviet advance long enough for the sappers to drop a bridge a few kilometres behind them. Only then would Gordon and his men be withdrawn to an assembly area to rest, rearm and reorganize. A few hours ago he would have acknowledge that order without hesitation. Now, however...

Hearing his captain wavering, the CO reminded him sharply of Clan Gordon's motto, 'Bydand', Stay and fight. 'Stay and fight,' Gordon muttered quietly to himself as he watched his men prepare to once more meet the Russians. 'Stay and bloody fight!' What had previously been a trite little motto was now the order of the day.

'Wilco, out.' Gordon at last wearily acknowledged the order before setting out to make sure the jocks still with him understood what was expected of them.

The 1st Queen's Dragoon Guards are a new regiment formed in 1959 by the amalgamation of the two senior cavalry regiments in the British Army: 1st King's Dragoon Guards and The Queen's Bays (2nd Dragoon Guards). Under various names these two regiments have been fighting for the Crown for three hundred years, since the Battle of the Boyne in 1690. Their long list of battle honours reflect their involvement in Britain's wars, both in Europe and throughout the Empire since then.

By the Second World War, both regiments had converted to armoured cars, leaving behind their horses for good. Often fighting side by side, the two (battalion-strength) armoured car regiments led the way for the Eighth Army throughout the war in North Africa and Italy.

With the post-war reductions in the size of the British Army, the two regiments became one, combining their illustrious histories as the 1st Queen's Dragoon Guards. Known as 'The Welsh Cavalry', the regiment has retained its reconnaissance role, serving in Borneo, Aden, and Lebanon.

When Britain mobilised for the current war, the regiment, equipped with the latest Scorpion and Scimitar tracked reconnaissance vehicles, hastened from its training grounds in Britain to rejoin its division. As the 3rd 'Iron Sides' Armoured Division's reconnaissance regiment, the Queen's Dragoon Guards rarely operated as a unit. Instead, each squadron spread out across its sector of the division's front to act as a trip line to detect the anticipated Soviet attack and determine the direction of the main thrust.

Although lightly equipped, there were times during the retreat to the Weser when the regiment was the only unit available. Massing its combat power, the regiment launched several successful counterattacks against the flanks of the Soviet advance.

MEDIUM RECCE SQUADRON

QUEEN'S DRAGOON GUARDS

SPARTAN RECCE SQUADRON HQ
TB110

2x Spartan — **1 POINT**

• TANK FORMATION • SCOUT •

COURAGE 3+	SKILL 2+
MORALE 3+	ASSAULT 3+
REMOUNT 4+	COUNTERATTACK 5+

IS HIT ON 4+

FRONT	SIDE	TOP
2	1	1

TACTICAL	TERRAIN DASH	CROSS COUNTRY DASH	ROAD DASH	CROSS
10"/25CM	20"/50CM	28"/70CM	36"/90CM	3+

WEAPON	RANGE	ROF HALTED	ROF MOVING	ANTI-TANK	FIRE-POWER	NOTES
7.62mm AA MG	16"/40CM	3	3	2	6	

QUEEN'S DRAGOON GUARDS

SCIMITAR RECCE TROOP
TB111

OR

QUEEN'S DRAGOON GUARDS

SCORPION RECCE TROOP
TB112

QUEEN'S DRAGOON GUARDS

SCIMITAR RECCE TROOP
TB111

OR

QUEEN'S DRAGOON GUARDS

SCORPION RECCE TROOP
TB112

QUEEN'S DRAGOON GUARDS

SCIMITAR RECCE TROOP
TB111

OR

QUEEN'S DRAGOON GUARDS

SCORPION RECCE TROOP
TB112

QUEEN'S DRAGOON GUARDS

STRIKER GUIDED WEAPONS TROOP
TB113

QUEEN'S DRAGOON GUARDS

SPARTAN SUPPORT TROOP
TB114

SCIMITAR RECCE TROOP

SCIMITAR RECCE TROOP	
4x Scimitar	**4 POINTS**
2x Scimitar	**2 POINTS**

The British Army Of the Rhine had three tracked reconnaissance regiments. The recce troops of the first two were equipped entirely with Scimitar reconnaissance vehicles, while the recce troops of the third mixed Scimitars and Scorpions together.

As divisional troops, the medium recce squadron's main role is to be a trip line to detect Soviet thrusts and identify the main effort ahead of the divisions main line of resistance, while denying Soviet reconnaissance troops the opportunity to identify where the British defences lie. A secondary role is to act as a mobile force to eliminate light Soviet forces airlanded behind the front line.

• TANK UNIT • INFRA-RED (IR) • SCOUT • SPEARHEAD •

COURAGE 4+	SKILL 3+
MORALE 4+	ASSAULT 3+
REMOUNT 4+	COUNTERATTACK 5+

IS HIT ON 4+

FRONT	SIDE	TOP
2	1	1

TACTICAL	TERRAIN DASH	CROSS COUNTRY DASH	ROAD DASH	CROSS
6"/15CM	20"/50CM	28"/70CM	36"/90CM	3+

WEAPON	RANGE	ROF HALTED	ROF MOVING	ANTI-TANK	FIRE-POWER	NOTES
30mm L21 Rarden gun	24"/60CM	3	2	10	5+	Sneak and Peek
7.62mm MG	16"/40CM	3	3	2	6	

Crew: 3 - commander/loader, gunner, driver
Weight: 7.8 tonnes
Length: 4.96m (16'3")
Width: 2.24m (7'4")
Height: 2.10m (6'11")

Weapons: 30mm L21 Rarden gun / 7.62mm L37 MG
Armour: 25mm Aluminium
Speed: 80 km/h (50 mph)
Engine: Jaguar J60, 140 kW (190 hp)
Range: 480 km (300 miles)

SCORPION RECCE TROOP

SCORPION RECCE TROOP	
4x Scorpion	**4 POINTS**
2x Scorpion	**2 POINTS**

The main difference between the Scorpion and the Scimitar is their main armament. The Scimitar mounts a 30mm L21 Rarden automatic gun with a high rate of fire, while the Scorpion mounts a 76mm L23 gun with a slower rate of fire, but a deadly HESH (High Explosive Squash Head) round that demolishes light armoured vehicles, buildings, and infantry bunkers with equal ease.

Being small and light, the Scorpion and Scimitar are exceedingly quick. However, that small size is achieved at the cost of having the commander load the main gun making it difficult to coordinate fire and movement.

• TANK UNIT • INFRA-RED (IR) • SCOUT • SPEARHEAD •

COURAGE 4+	SKILL 3+
MORALE 4+	ASSAULT 3+
REMOUNT 4+	COUNTERATTACK 5+

IS HIT ON 4+

FRONT	SIDE	TOP
2	1	1

TACTICAL	TERRAIN DASH	CROSS COUNTRY DASH	ROAD DASH	CROSS
6"/15CM	20"/50CM	28"/70CM	36"/90CM	3+

WEAPON	RANGE	ROF HALTED	ROF MOVING	ANTI-TANK	FIRE-POWER	NOTES
76mm L23 gun	24"/60CM	2	1	14	2+	HEAT, Smoke, Sneak and Peek
7.62mm MG	16"/40CM	3	3	2	6	

Crew: 3 - commander/loader, gunner, driver
Weight: 7.9 tonnes
Length: 4.79m (15'9")
Width: 2.24m (7'4")
Height: 2.10m (6'11")

Weapons: 76mm L23 gun / 7.62mm L37 MG
Armour: 25mm Aluminium
Speed: 80 km/h (50 mph)
Engine: Jaguar J60, 140 kW (190 hp)
Range: 480 km (300 miles)

STRIKER GUIDED WEAPONS TROOP

STRIKER GUIDED WEAPONS TROOP	
4x Striker	**10 POINTS**
2x Striker	**5 POINTS**

The FV102 Striker provides the armoured reconnaissance regiment with long-range heavy anti-tank capability. Mounting five Swingfire missiles on the Spartan chassis, the Striker punches far above its weight.

Like the armoured regiment's FV438 Swingfire, the gunner of the Striker can dismount and move away from his hidden vehicle to fire. Combined with a very low profile, this makes the Striker hard to counter. Often avoiding its field of fire is the safest solution, but with such a long range, that isn't easy to do.

TACTICAL	TERRAIN DASH	CROSS COUNTRY DASH	ROAD DASH	CROSS
10"/25cm	20"/50cm	28"/70cm	36"/90cm	3+

WEAPON	RANGE	ROF HALTED	MOVING	ANTI-TANK	FIRE-POWER	NOTES
Swingfire missile	8"/20cm–48"/120cm	1	-	23	3+	Guided, HEAT
7.62mm AA MG	16"/40cm	3	3	2	6	

Crew: 3 - commander, gunner, driver
Weight: 8.3 tonnes
Length: 4.83m (15' 10")
Width: 2.24m (7' 4")
Height: 2.21m (7' 3")

Weapons: Swingfire guided missiles
7.62mm L7 MG
Armour: 25mm Aluminium
Speed: 80 km/h (50 mph)
Engine: Jaguar J60, 140 kW (190 hp)

Laying flat on his stomach, letting the early morning dew soak through his combats was not the best way to greet a new dawn. Unfortunately, Sergeant John Bartlett had no choice. No. 2 Section's newly promoted corporal desperately needed him, if for no other reason than to steady the lad for the task at hand as a scene that would have unnerved Old Hookey himself unfolded before them at a range of just over four thousand meters.

"You need to be patient son," Bartlett murmured reassuringly. "It's best if we let the gentlemen begin to deploy, catching them on their back foot. With luck, by the time they manage to sort themselves out, the squadron will be on its way back to their next position leaving us free to pack up and follow."

"Which one do we take out?" the young corporal asked in a tone of voice several octaves higher than that which Bartlett was accustomed to hearing.

Looking over to where No. 2 Section's FV102 Striker sat, nestled in a hollow just behind the rise, Bartlett took in a deep breath before looking back at the column of Soviet tanks that were uncoiling from march column and into line of battle. "Not long, corporal. Not long. Just remember, you have one shot, so do what the lieutenant told you, look for the tank that's doing something different. Odds are, he'll be an officer."

"And if we can't find him?"

Despite the situation, Bartlett chuckled. "Then give the bloke in the lead what for. That'll cause everyone behind him to think twice about charging out and being a bleedin' hero."

"Right," the corporal muttered. "Makes sense."

Yeah, Bartlett thought to himself as they went back to watching the Soviet tanks close on their position. Let's hope it actually works.

SPARTAN SUPPORT TROOP

SPARTAN SUPPORT TROOP	
4x GPMG team with 66mm anti-tank	
4x Spartan [TB115]	**4 POINTS**
3x GPMG team with 66mm anti-tank	
3x Spartan [TB115]	**3 POINTS**

• INFANTRY UNIT •

COURAGE 4+	SKILL 3+
MORALE 4+	ASSAULT 3+
RALLY 4+	COUNTERATTACK 3+

IS HIT ON	INFANTRY SAVE
4+	**3+**

TACTICAL	TERRAIN DASH	CROSS COUNTRY DASH	ROAD DASH	CROSS
8"/20CM	8"/20CM	12"/30CM	12"/30CM	AUTO

WEAPON	RANGE	ROF HALTED	ROF MOVING	ANTI-TANK	FIRE-POWER	NOTES
GPMG team	16"/40CM	3	2	2	6	
or 66mm anti-tank	12"/30CM	1	1	12	5+	*HEAT, Slow Firing*

Each recce squadron has a small infantry component called the Support Troop. Their roles are many and varied, ranging from clearing enemy-held woods and villages to allow the rest of the squadron through, to defending those same woods and villages against enemy probes.

The Support Troop is armed with the standard GPMG (General Purpose Machine-gun) based on the excellent Belgian FN MAG design, the L1A1 SLR (Self-Loading Rifle), and 66mm anti-tank rockets (known as the M72 LAW in US service). This light armament allows them to move quickly, while still being ready to tackle enemy infantry and their supporting BMP fighting vehicles .

SPARTAN TRANSPORT

The Support Troop is mounted in FV103 Spartan armoured personnel carriers based on the same Scorpion chassis as the rest of the squadron. These give them the speed and protection to get into position ahead of the enemy in time to prepare a hot reception.

The Spartan's light aluminium armour actually provides better protection for its passengers than the heavier, though thinner, steel armour of the infantry's standard FV432 APC.

• TANK ATTACHMENT • PASSENGERS 1 •

COURAGE 4+	SKILL 3+
MORALE 4+	ASSAULT 4+
REMOUNT 4+	COUNTERATTACK 5+

IS HIT ON 4+		
FRONT	SIDE	TOP
2	1	1

TACTICAL	TERRAIN DASH	CROSS COUNTRY DASH	ROAD DASH	CROSS
10"/25CM	20"/50CM	28"/70CM	36"/90CM	3+

WEAPON	RANGE	ROF HALTED	ROF MOVING	ANTI-TANK	FIRE-POWER	NOTES
7.62mm AA MG	16"/40CM	3	3	2	6	

QUEEN'S DRAGOON GUARDS

An amateur historian, Captain Andy Webb was familiar with most military truisms. His particular favourite was that in war, timing was everything. As the Battery Captain of the Gibraltar Battery, he was in charge of eight Abbot self-propelled guns. Webb knew that giving the order for his unit to relocate too soon during a fighting withdrawal would leave the forward units he was supporting bereft of fire support just when they needed it the most. However, wait too long and the guns would find themselves where they didn't belong, on the very forward edge of the battlefield.

Watching in horror as tank after tank emerged from the forest on the far side of the valley, a mere kilometre from his battery's position, Webb knew he'd waited too long. There was no time to wonder how they had managed to get that far into the battle group's rear without anyone reporting them. All he and his gun crews could do now was to give as good an account for themselves as they could.

'Action Tanks!' he shouted. Along the entire gun line, from left to right, ammo handlers rushed anti-tank rounds forward to each gun's No. 2. No one bothered cutting the charges. There simply wasn't any time to. Loaders rammed home whatever round they were handed even as their gun's No. 3 furiously cranked the elevation and traverse wheels of their guns, laying on the first tank that appeared in their sights.

With his crews doing all they could as quickly as was humanly possible to engage the Russian tanks, Webb hastily studied the map in front of him. Jabbing a grimy finger on a spot that lay between his guns and the Russians, he issued a call for fire to other batteries located further to the rear. 'Fire Mission Division, Grid 482 642, Tank Battalion, Fire For Effect!'

The wait seemed endless. Several Soviet tanks were burning, but two of his own guns were blazing wrecks when the small stream along the valley floor erupted just as the lead tanks started crossing. Even at this distance, the effect was a body blow as battery after battery turned the valley floor into an inferno.

IRON DIVISION
ABBOT FIELD BATTERY

ABBOT FIELD BATTERY	
8x Abbot	**12 POINTS**
4x Abbot	**6 POINTS**
2x Abbot	**3 POINTS**

Crew: 4 - commander, gunner, loader, driver
Weight: 16.6 tonnes
Length: 5.84m (32')
Width: 2.64m (12')
Height: 2.49m (8')
Weapons: 105mm L13 gun, 7.62mm L4 MG
Armour: 13mm
Speed: 48 km/h (30 mph)
Engine: Rolls-Royce K60, 180 kW (240 hp)

TACTICAL	TERRAIN DASH	CROSS COUNTRY DASH	ROAD DASH	CROSS
10"/25CM	14"/35CM	20"/50CM	24"/60CM	3+

WEAPON	RANGE	ROF HALTED	ROF MOVING	ANTI-TANK	FIRE-POWER	NOTES
105mm L13 gun	88"/220CM	ARTILLERY		4	4+	Smoke Bombardment
or Direct fire	28"/70CM	1	1	17	1+	Brutal, HEAT, Slow Firing, Smoke
7.62mm AA MG	16"/40CM	3	3	2	6	

The FV433 Abbot self-propelled gun mounts a 105mm gun on a modified FV432 armoured personnel carrier chassis. Although its calibre is relatively small for a modern artillery piece, the 105mm gun fires a high-capacity shell that gives it an excellent performance.

The Abbot provides close support for the armoured brigades, where its presence is much appreciated. The guns are very effective against infantry and light armour, as well as providing smoke screens to mask the defenders from enemy fire while repositioning.

IRON DIVISION
M109 FIELD BATTERY

M109 FIELD BATTERY

8x M109	**20 POINTS**
4x M109	**10 POINTS**
2x M109	**5 POINTS**

The divisional artillery has replaced the Abbot with the American M109 with its 155mm gun. This powerful weapon is called upon when some serious firepower is needed.

• TANK UNIT •

COURAGE 4+	SKILL 3+
MORALE 4+	ASSAULT 4+
REMOUNT 4+	COUNTERATTACK 5+

IS HIT ON 4+

FRONT	SIDE	TOP
2	2	1

TACTICAL	TERRAIN DASH	CROSS COUNTRY DASH	ROAD DASH	CROSS
10"/25CM	16"/40CM	24"/60CM	28"/70CM	3+

WEAPON	RANGE	ROF HALTED	ROF MOVING	ANTI-TANK	FIRE-POWER	NOTES
M185 155mm howitzer	96"/240CM	ARTILLERY		4	2+	Smoke Bombardment
or Direct fire	36"/90CM	1	1	15	1+	Brutal, Slow Firing, Smoke
7.62mm AA MG	16"/40CM	3	3	2	6	

IRON DIVISION
FV432 FOO

FORWARD OBSERVATION OFFICER

1x FV432 FOO	**1 POINT**

You must field:
- *an Iron Division Abbot Field Battery [TB120], or*
- *an Iron Division M109 Field Battery [TB121], or*
- *an Irish Guards FV432 Mortar Platoon [TB107] before you may field an Iron Division FV432 FOO.*

• INDEPENDENT TANK UNIT • OBSERVER • SCOUT • THERMAL IMAGING •

COURAGE 4+	SKILL 3+
MORALE 4+	ASSAULT 4+
REMOUNT 4+	COUNTERATTACK 5+

IS HIT ON 4+

FRONT	SIDE	TOP
1	1	1

TACTICAL	TERRAIN DASH	CROSS COUNTRY DASH	ROAD DASH	CROSS
10"/25CM	16"/40CM	20"/50CM	24"/60CM	3+

WEAPON	RANGE	ROF HALTED	ROF MOVING	ANTI-TANK	FIRE-POWER	NOTES
7.62mm AA MG	16"/40CM	3	3	2	6	

SPARTAN BLOWPIPE SAM SECTION

SPARTAN BLOWPIPE SAM SECTION	
6x Spartan (Blowpipe)	**9 POINTS**
4x Spartan (Blowpipe)	**6 POINTS**
2x Spartan (Blowpipe)	**3 POINTS**

The Blowpipe man-portable anti-aircraft missile is somewhat unique in that it is not self-homing. The operator pilots the missile until it intercepts the target. This requires a lot of skill to do successfully, but does make it immune to countermeasures like jamming, chaff, and flares.

This method of operation has another benefit too. With a bit of cleverness, the operator can also engage ground targets with the missile, as demonstrated when they were used against bunkers in the Falklands War.

• TANK UNIT • INFRA-RED (IR) •

COURAGE 4+	SKILL 3+
MORALE 4+	ASSAULT 4+
REMOUNT 4+	COUNTERATTACK 5+

IS HIT ON 4+		
FRONT	SIDE	TOP
2	1	1

TACTICAL	TERRAIN DASH	CROSS COUNTRY DASH	ROAD DASH	CROSS
10"/25CM	20"/50CM	28"/70CM	36"/90CM	3+

WEAPON	RANGE	ROF HALTED	ROF MOVING	ANTI-TANK	FIRE-POWER	NOTES
Blowpipe AA missile	48"/120CM	2	-	-	4+	*Guided AA*
or Firing at Tanks and Infantry	16"/40CM-32"/80CM	1	-	12	4+	*Guided, HEAT*
7.62mm AA MG	16"/40CM	3	3	2	6	

TRACKED RAPIER SAM SECTION

TRACKED RAPIER SAM SECTION	
4x Tracked Rapier	**6 POINTS**
2x Tracked Rapier	**3 POINTS**

Tracked Rapier is a self-propelled version of the excellent Rapier surface-to-air missile (SAM) mounted on the chassis of a modified American M548 tracked carrier.

Typical of British missiles, the Rapier is not a homing missile, instead the commander tracks the target using a helmet-mounted sight, and the launcher sends signals to the missile to steer it on to the target. Like the Blowpipe, the result is a missile that is very hard to avoid.

Rapier has another twist in that it does not have a proximity fuse to detonate it in case of a near miss. The weight saving allows for a more manoeuvrable missile that is extremely deadly when it scores the required direct hit.

• TANK UNIT • INFRA-RED (IR) •

COURAGE 4+	SKILL 3+
MORALE 4+	ASSAULT -
REMOUNT 4+	COUNTERATTACK -

IS HIT ON 4+		
FRONT	SIDE	TOP
1	1	1

TACTICAL	TERRAIN DASH	CROSS COUNTRY DASH	ROAD DASH	CROSS
10"/25CM	14"/35CM	20"/50CM	24"/60CM	3+

WEAPON	RANGE	ROF HALTED	ROF MOVING	ANTI-TANK	FIRE-POWER	NOTES
Rapier missile	64"/160CM	3	-	-	3+	*Guided AA*

Crew:	*3- commander, operator, driver*	*Weapons:*	*Rapier guided AA missile*
Weight:	*14 tonnes*	*Armour:*	*25mm Aluminium*
Length:	*6.40m (21)*	*Speed:*	*48 km/h (30 mph)*
Width:	*2.80m (9'2")*	*Engine:*	*Detroit 6V-53, 157 kW (210 hp)*
Height:	*2.78m (9'1")*	*Range:*	*300 km (185 miles)*

IRON-DIVISION SUPPORT

IRON DIVISION
TOW LYNX HELARM FLIGHT

• HELICOPTER AIRCRAFT UNIT • **• HUNTER-KILLER • INFRA-RED (IR) •**

TOW LYNX HELARM FLIGHT	
4x TOW Lynx	**12 POINTS**
2x TOW Lynx	**6 POINTS**

COURAGE 4+	SKILL 3+
MORALE 4+	

IS HIT ON	AIRCRAFT SAVE
4+	**5+**

The TOW Lynx mounts the US Improved TOW anti-tank missile for the HELARM (Helicopter, Armed) operations. The Lynx is fast and aerobatic, making it ideal for the anti-tank role as it can fly below tree-top level to sneak into position, then pop up using its roof-mounted sights to acquire targets and destroy them with its missiles. Once done, the helicopter quickly repositions to avoid unwanted attention from Soviet air-defence vehicles.

TACTICAL	TERRAIN DASH	CROSS COUNTRY DASH	ROAD DASH	CROSS
UNLIMITED				AUTO

WEAPON	RANGE	ROF HALTED	ROF MOVING	ANTI-TANK	FIRE-POWER	NOTES
Improved TOW missile	8"/20CM–48"/120CM	1	-	21	3+	Guided, HEAT

Crew: 2 – pilot, co-pilot
Weight: 5.3 tonnes
Length: 15.24m (50')
Rotor: 12..80m (42')

Armour: None
Speed: 324 km/h (200 mph)
Engine: Rolls-Royce Gem turboshaft, 835 kW (1,120 hp)

IRON DIVISION
HARRIER CLOSE AIR SUPPORT FLIGHT

• STRIKE AIRCRAFT UNIT • JUMP JET •

HARRIER CLOSE AIR SUPPORT FLIGHT	
4x Harrier	**10 POINTS**
2x Harrier	**5 POINTS**

COURAGE 4+	SKILL 3+
MORALE 4+	

IS HIT ON	AIRCRAFT SAVE
4+	**5+**

The Hawker-Siddley Harrier, the famed 'Jump Jet' could swivel its exhaust nozzles down to allow it to take off vertically. The RAF use this capability to base the Harrier out of supermarket car parks and other concealed locations close to the front, reducing the interference from Soviet aircraft and allowing a higher sortie rate than conventional aircraft.

Armed with a electrically-powered 30mm Aden 5-chamber revolver cannon and BL-755 anti-tank cluster bombs, the Harrier is deadly against both air and ground targets.

TACTICAL	TERRAIN DASH	CROSS COUNTRY DASH	ROAD DASH	CROSS
UNLIMITED				AUTO

WEAPON	RANGE	ROF HALTED	ROF MOVING	ANTI-TANK	FIRE-POWER	NOTES
30mm Aden gun	8"/20CM	-	3	7	5+	Anti-helicopter
BL-755 cluster bombs	6"/15CM	SALVO		8	3+	

Crew: 1 – pilot
Empty: 6.1 tonnes
Loaded: 11.4 tonnes
Length: 14.27m (46' 10")
Wingspan: 7.70m (25'3")
Wing Area: 18.68m² (201 ft²)

Weapon: 30mm Aden cannon
Armour: None
Speed: 1175 km/h (730 mph)
Engine: RR Pegasus 103 turbofan, 96 kN (21,500lbf) thrust
Range: 370 km (230 miles)

"Fly high and die." The sight of his section leader's Harrier being swatted down by an SA-6 had been more than enough to convince Flying Officer Daren McGrievy that it was sound advice. Hugging the ground at treetop level while cruising along at eight-hundred-plus kilometres per hour, a pilot needed to pay full attention to what he was doing, lest he and the terrain he was skimming along suddenly became one.

After making his last turn toward the east, McGrievy contacted the forward air controller who had eyes on his target, a pontoon bridge. "Echo 25, this is Fox 17, IP now. Confirm Alpha Mike."

"Fox 17, I confirm Bravo. Clear to engage, nil 1,000."

No friendlies within a thousand metres. That was good. Just Russians, and lots of them.

Once over the last tree covered rise, he realized just how right he'd been, for they were there, cued up bumper to bumper on the east bank of the river crossing like eager holiday motorists fighting their way along the M4.

"Tally ho," McGrievy muttered to himself as he made a quick jink to the right and lined up for his final run in, ignoring the hail of angry tracers coming his way from every tank and ZSU that could be brought to bear.

"Steady lad," he murmured as sweat trickling down from under his helmet began to sting his eyes. "Steady."

"NOW!" he almost screamed to himself as he pickled his BL-755 cluster bombs and jinked hard again.

Over the radio he heard the FAC call out. "Splash on target. Standby for BDA."

"Standby my arse," McGrievy growled as he jinked left, then right, then left again. "I'm out of here, mate."

The British Army has a number of unusual features. These are reflected in the following special rules.

BAZOOKA SKIRTS

After seeing the effectiveness of German 'bazookas' in the Second World War, the British fitted all of their post-war battle tanks with 'bazooka skirts', spaced armour to protect them from light, hand-held anti-tank weapons.

> Teams with Bazooka Skirts have a side armour rating of 10 against HEAT weapons.

JUMP JET

The Harrier jump jet can get airborne with a full armament load after a short take-off run. This allows it to operate from hidden locations near the front, like supermarket car parks, enabling them to quickly rearm and return to the front after a sortie.

> Jump Jet Strike Aircraft arrive each turn on a roll of 3+, rather than the usual 4+.

OVERHEAD FIRE

Despite being used by their grandfathers fighting in Germany back in WWII, the 2" mortar gives the squaddies good service as a grenade launcher firing both smoke and explosive rounds. It's arcing fire allows it to shoot over friendly troops as they attack.

> A 2" mortar team can shoot over friendly teams.

SNEAK AND PEEK

The Scorpion and Scimitar are designed to find the enemy, not fight them. If it comes to a scrap, they prefer a quick ambush and an equally quick departure. As the tank commander also doubles as the main gun's loader, it is tricky to manoeuvre when firing the main gun, so the gunner can only fire the co-ax machine-gun when advancing at speed.

> A tank with Sneak and Peek can move 10"/25cm at Tactical if it is not firing its main gun

SWINGFIRE

The Swingfire anti-tank guided missile has several unique features. The first, which gave it its name, is the ability to 'swing' up to 90 degrees on launch, giving it an impressive field of fire from a fixed launcher. The second is the capability for the missile controller to be dismounted and moved up to 50m from the firing vehicle. These features allow the launch vehicle to remain hidden while firing.

> A Team firing Swingfire missiles can remain Gone to Ground while shooting.

With the squadron commander's Spartan burning furiously on the road next to the church and contact with regiment spotty due to jamming, Captain Moran realized it was up to him to decide when to break contact. They'd rehearsed doing this time and again during map exercises back in garrison. Yet even then, it had always been a tricky affair, with decisions based more on guesswork than a clear, concise assessment of the situation. Doing so under fire, with the Russians ready to pounce on them the second they realized the squadron was pulling out would be 'interesting'. One mistake would be deadly.

After a quick glance down at the map laid out on the roof of his Spartan, he decided 1 Troop would be the next to go. It was not only the most exposed, the lieutenant commanding it was, in his opinion, on the verge of cracking under the stress of probes by Russian infantry who were infesting the woods on the squadron's left.

If that troop was to stand any chance of escaping, 4 Troop's Strikers would have to suppress the Russian tanks in the woods from its position in the village.

"Right," the 2IC murmured to himself under his breath. "Let's see if we can make this…"

The whine of incoming artillery caused the 2IC to drop down into the turret of his Scimitar, putting an end to both his mutterings and his preparations for the moment.

COVERING FORCE

When the war broke out, A Squadron of the 1st Queen's Dragoon Guards was tasked with delaying the Soviet advance on Schellerten along the Midland Canal while the rest of the division deployed to its wartime positions. The forward detachment of the leading Soviet motor rifle regiment attempted to brush their defence aside and reach the main battle area before the British could prepare their defence.

SPECIAL RULES
- Ambush (page 100 of *Team Yankee*)
- Dawn (page 98 of *Team Yankee*)
- Covering Force

COVERING FORCE

The British covering force is only there to delay the Soviet advance, not to fight to the death. As the fight progresses they must progressively disengage their forces and retire to the main line of resistance.

At the start of their turns *three*, *five*, and *seven*, the British player removes a Unit (all of its teams and any Attachments) from the table. If the selected Unit is not in Good Spirits (see page 64 of *Team Yankee*) and has a Team within 8"/20cm of an enemy Team, roll a die before removing the Unit.
- If the score is at least equal to the Unit's Skill number, they successfully withdraw, ready to fight again later.
- Otherwise, the whole Unit is Destroyed as it is removed.

At the start of their turns *six* and *seven* the British player removes one of the Objectives. Since this happens in the British turn, the Objectives won't be there in the Soviet player's turn when it comes time to check whether they have won. This makes it possible for the British player to steal victory out from the Soviet player's grasp, so the forward detachment needs to move quickly and secure the objectives before they can be removed.

SETTING UP

Lay out the terrain on a 6' x 4' (180cm x 120cm) table as shown on the map on the following page. Place three Objectives on the spots marked ●.

DEPLOYMENT

The British player holds one Unit in Ambush. They then place their remaining Units in their half of the table. The infantry of the Spartan Support Troop may start the game in Foxholes.

The Soviet player then places all of their Units within 8"/20cm of their table edge.

STARTING THE GAME

The game starts at Dawn (see page 98 of *Team Yankee*). The Soviet player is the Attacker and has the first turn.

WINNING THE GAME

The Soviet player wins if they start a turn Holding one of the Objectives (be aware that the British player will be removing two of the Objectives during the game).

Otherwise, the British player wins at the start of their eighth turn after checking Formation Morale if necessary.

CONSEQUENCES

If the British covering force wins, they have bought time for their main force to deploy, giving them more troops at the start of their next battle.

If the Soviet forward detachment wins, they brush aside the covering force and arrive before the British are ready, reducing the size of the British force at the start of the next battle.

WHAT HAPPENED

The covering force held on, but only just. Their losses were high, reducing their effectiveness for the rest of the campaign.

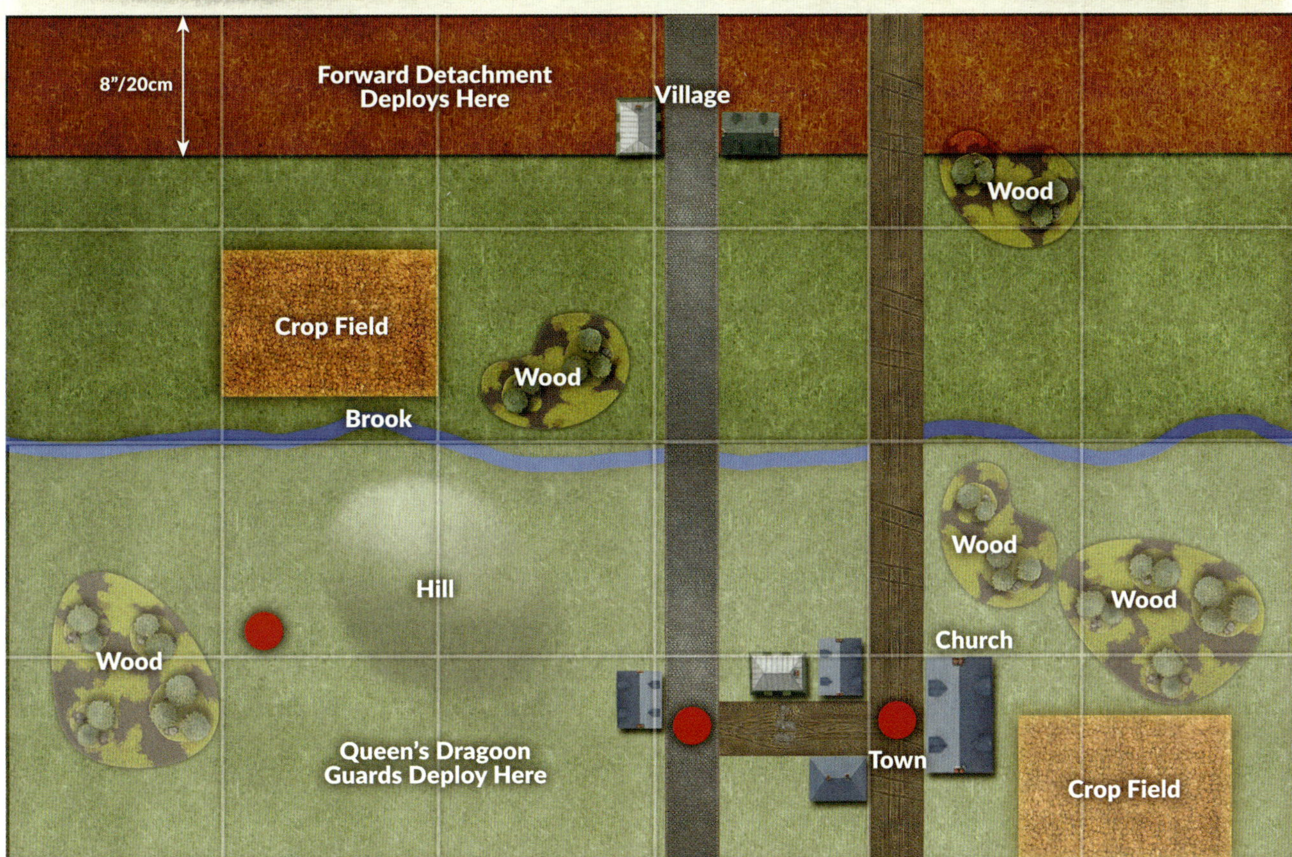

FORCES

QUEEN'S DRAGOON GUARDS

Medium Recce Squadron HQ
    2x Spartan

3x Scorpion Recce Troops (each)
    4x Scorpion

Striker Guided Weapons Troop
    4x Striker

Spartan Support Troop
    4x GPMG team with 66mm anti-tank
    4x Spartan

Chieftain Armoured Troop
    3x Chieftain

ALTERNATIVE FORCE: 45 POINTS

FORWARD DETACHMENT

T-72 Tank Battalion HQ
    1x T-72

3x T-72 Tank Companies (each)
    3x T-72

BMP-2 Motor Rifle Company
    4x AK-74 team with RPG-18 anti-tank
    3x RPG-7 anti-tank team
    4x BMP-2

2x BMP-2 Recon Platoons (each)
    4x BMP-2

ALTERNATIVE FORCE: 60 POINTS

The covering force has done its job and it's time for the main event. The leading elements of the Death or Glory Boys are in position to defend the outskirts of Shellerten. The Soviet main body needs to break through their position before they can be reinforced to stop them.

SPECIAL RULES

- Ambush (page 96 of *Team Yankee*)
- Deep Immediate Reserve (page 101 of *Team Yankee*)

SETTING UP

Lay out the terrain on a 6' x 4' (180cm x 120cm) table as shown on the map on the following page. Place three Objectives on the spots marked ●.

DEPLOYMENT

The British player holds one Unit in Ambush. They then place the remaining Units of their initial force in their half of the table. The infantry of the FV432 Mechanised Platoon may start the game in Foxholes.

They then place four Minefield markers in their table half or up to 16"/40cm into the Soviet table half.

The rest of their force will arrive from Immediate Reserve (page 101 of *Team Yankee*) from their table edge as the game progresses.

The Soviet player then places all of their Units in their table half, at least 16"/40cm back from the table centre line.

STARTING THE GAME

The Soviet player is the Attacker and has the first turn.

WINNING THE GAME

The Soviet player wins if they start a turn Holding one of the Objectives.

The British player wins if they start any turn on or after their sixth turn with no Soviet tanks or infantry in their half of the table.

CAMPAIGN

If the British player won the Covering Force scenario, they have bought time for the reserves to get closer to the front. The British player gets Reserves on a roll of 4+ on their first turn.

If the Soviet player won the Covering Force scenario, they have bulled through the covering force before the main defences are ready. The British player may only place two Minefield markers at the start of the game.

CONSEQUENCES

If the British win, the first echelon of the Soviet attack has been blunted. They'll commit more forces to force a break-through, but they'll keep paying heavily for every inch of ground they take.

If the Soviet main body wins, they will continue their advance, pushing deep into the British defences. The British will have to scramble to stop them, meanwhile more and more troops will be flooding through the gap you have made.

WHAT HAPPENED

The British defenders halted the first echelon's assault before breaking off and falling back to their next defensive position under heavy pressure from the next wave of Soviet forces.

THE NEXT STEP

The Team Yankee website has a third scenario covering the fighting for bridge at Heinde and suggestions on how all three battles can be combined on a single table.

Go to *www.Team-Yankee.com/IronMaidenScenarios*.

BRITISH FORCES

DEATH OR GLORY BOYS

Chieftain Armoured Squadron HQ
- 1x Chieftain Stillbrew

Chieftain Armoured Troop
- 3x Chieftain Stillbrew

Swingfire Guided Weapons Troop
- 3x Swingfire

FV432 Mechanised Platoon
- 4x GPMG team with 66mm anti-tank
- 3x Carl Gustav anti-tank team
- 1x 2" mortar team
- 2x Milan missile team
- 5x FV432

Abbot Field Battery
- 4x Abbot

FV432 FOO

DEEP IMMEDIATE RESERVES

Chieftain Armoured Troop
- 3x Chieftain Stillbrew

Chieftain Armoured Troop
- 2x Chieftain

Scorpion Recce Troop
- 2x Scorpion

Spartan Blowpipe SAM Section
- 2x Spartan Blowpipe

Lynx HELARM Flight
- 2x TOW Lynx

Harrier Close Air Support Flight
- 2x Harrier

ALTERNATIVE FORCE: 100 POINTS
AT LEAST 50 POINTS MUST START IN RESERVE

SCENARIOS

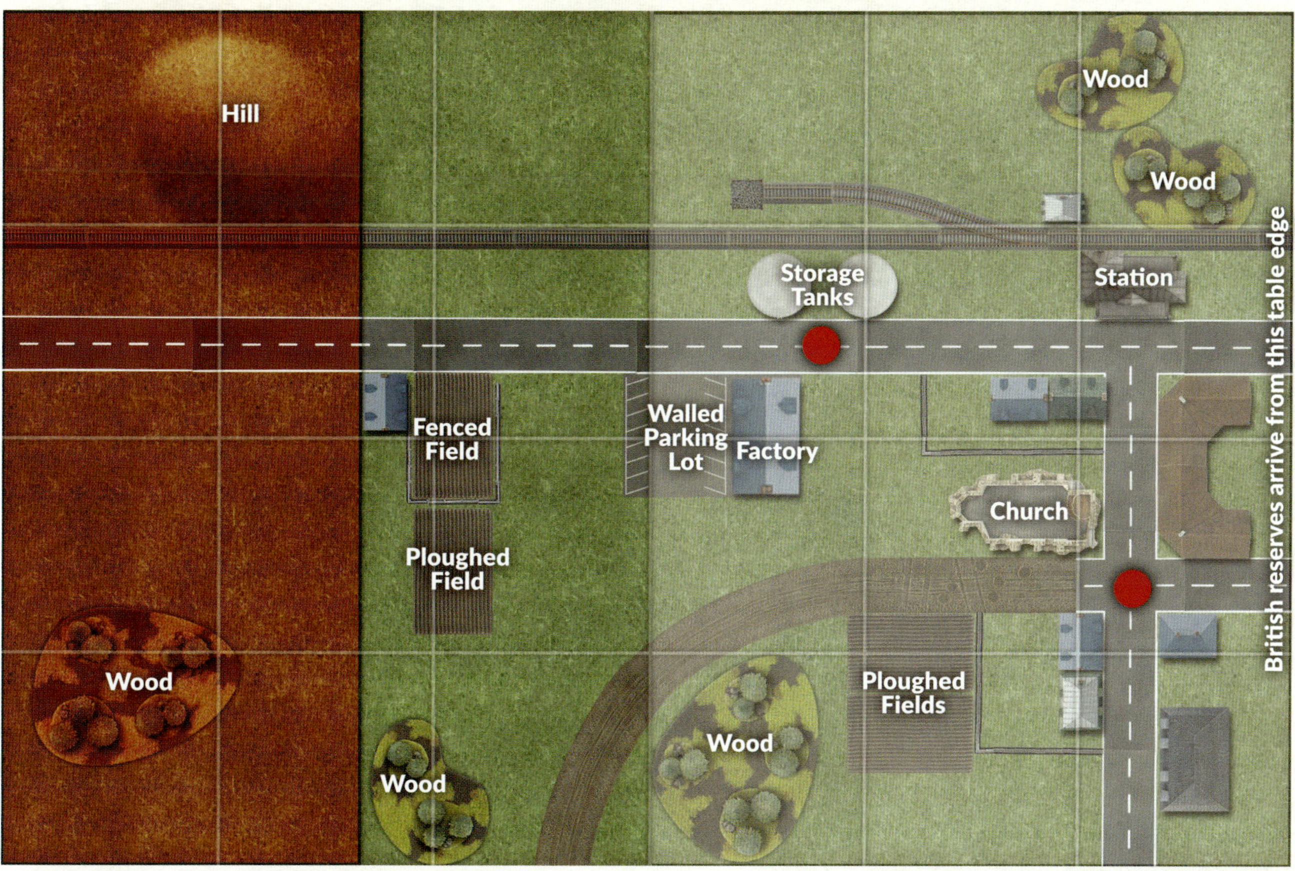

SOVIET FORCES

MAIN BODY

T-72 Tank Battalion HQ
 1x T-72

T-72 Tank Company
 6x T-72 (3 with Mine Clearing Devices)

T-72 Tank Company
 6x T-72 (2 with Mine Clearing Devices)

BMP-2 Motor Rifle Company
 7x AK-74 team with RPG-18 anti-tank
 6x RPG-7 anti-tank team
 2x PKM LMG team
 9x BMP-2

ZSU-23-4 AA Platoon
 2x ZSU-23-4

SA-13 Gopher SAM Platoon
 2x SA-13 Gopher

2S1 Carnation SP Howitzer Battery
 3x 2S1 Carnation

Mi-24 Hind Assault Helicopter Company
 2x Mi-24 Hind

SU-25 Frogfoot Aviation Company
 2xSU-25 Frogfoot

ALTERNATIVE FORCE: 100 POINTS

BRITISH ARMOUR

CHIEFTAIN
STILLBREW

In the mid 1980s, the British Army uparmoured their Chieftain tanks with the Stillbrew armour package. The most notable part of this is the thick layer of armour added to the turret front.

BRITISH AIRCRAFT

PAINTING BRITISH FORCES

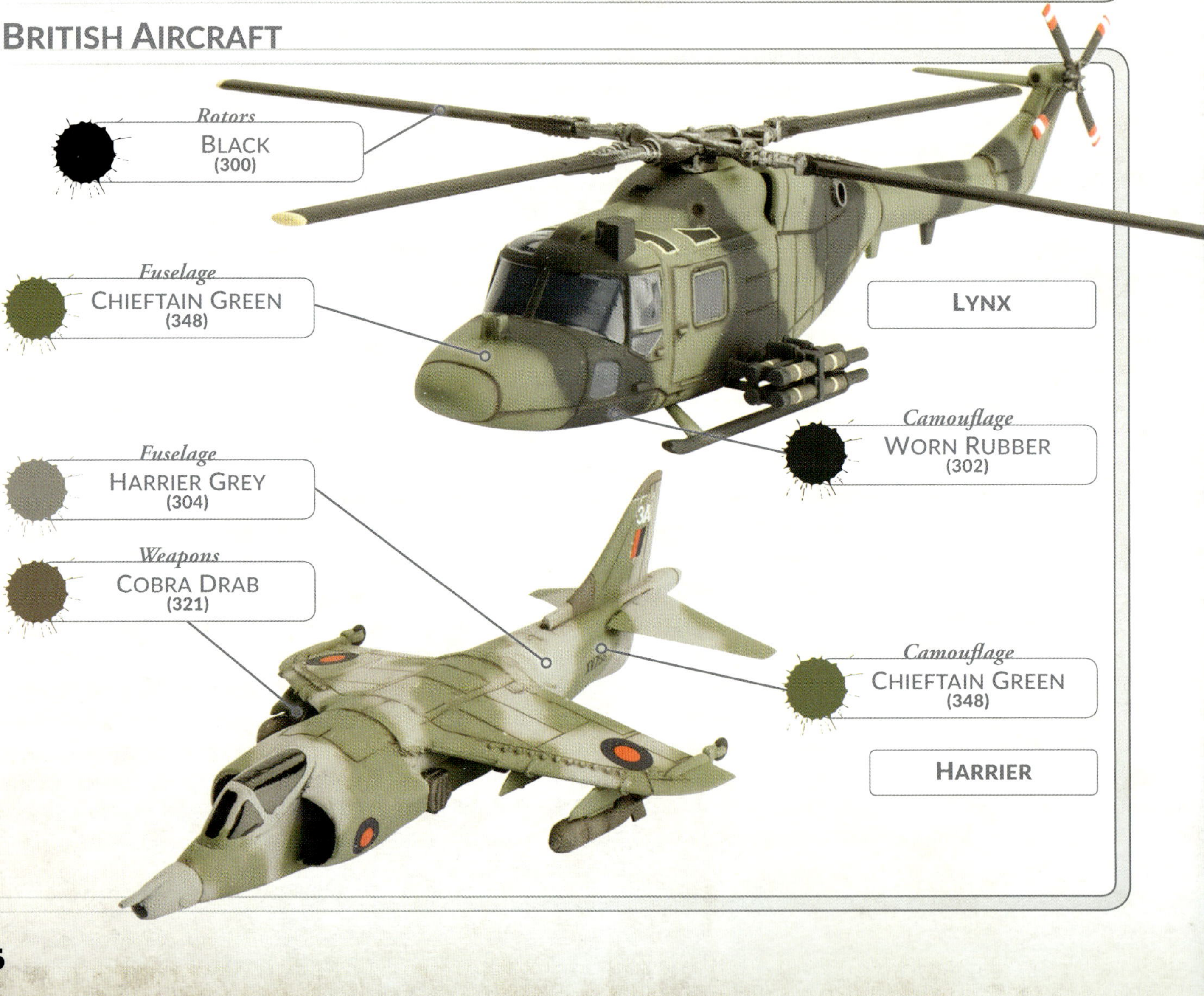

BAOR Camouflage

PAINTING BRITISH FORCES

Colour Palette

Chieftain Green
(348)

Battlefield Brown
(324)

Worn Rubber
(302)

Ordnance Shade
(492)

Maverick Khaki
(346)

Comrade Khaki
(326)

Dry Dust
(364)

The British Army used a black on green camouflage scheme for its tanks and helicopters. This simple scheme disrupted the outline of the tank in the dappled light at the edge of a wood or other ambush position.

CHIEFTAIN GREEN
Large Brush

BASECOAT *your tank with Chieftain Green. Two thin coats are preferable to one thick coat. Alternatively you can use a Chieftain Green spray can for your undercoat.*

BATTLEFIELD BROWN
Medium Brush

BASECOAT *the wheels and hull surfaces with Chieftain Green and paint the tracks Battlefield Brown.*

WORN RUBBER
Large Brush

CAMOUFLAGE *with Worn Rubber in random wavy stripes.*

WORN RUBBER
Medium Brush

WASH *the tracks with Ordnance Shade and paint the road wheels and track pads with Worn Rubber.*

MAVERICK KHAKI
Medium Brush

HIGHLIGHT *the edges with a dry brush of Maverick Khaki.*

COMRADE KHAKI
Fine Brush

PAINT *the thermal sleeve on the barrel with Comrade Khaki then wash with Ordnance Shade. Dry brush with Comrade Khaki.*

DRY DUST
Drybrush

DRYBRUSH *the tank with Dry Dust concentrating on skirts, wheels, and tracks to simulate accumulated dust.*

ORDNANCE SHADE
Fine Brush

WASH *the details with Ordnance Shade to add definition.*

This painting guide uses the *Colours Of War* painting system. *Colours of War* book is a detailed and comprehensive guide to painting miniatures that shows you, step-by-step, everything you need to know to field beautifully painted miniatures in your *Team Yankee* games. While *Colours of War* focuses on the Second World War miniatures of *Flames Of War*, the techniques work just the same for *Team Yankee*.

Visit the *Team Yankee* website: www.Team-Yankee.com for more information.

The Times
Thursday 8 August:

The British Army's withdrawal from the border with East Germany has been conducted according to the planned timetable according to statements from NATO headquarters. Soviet losses have been high as they have attempted unsuccessfully to force the British Army back at a faster pace.

Reports of a Soviet breakthrough around Hamburg have been dismissed by NATO headquarters as 'unfounded', although German and Dutch forces have been forced to 'withdraw at a faster rate than planned in this area'. NATO

headquarters has stated that 'the exchange rate has been highly favourable' and that the Soviet armies will 'soon run out of steam'.

The Guardian
Saturday 10 August:

The successful withdrawal from the West German border to the main line of defence along the Weser River and the Mittland Canal has been successfully completed according to NATO Headquarters. This difficult operation by the British Army has put the centre of the NATO line into a secure defensive position in line with pre-war planning.

While Soviet forces continue to make headway in the North German Plain, the British position astride the central axis provides a solid foundation for a future counterattack. NATO headquarters are unable to release information about the timing or location of the projected counterattack, but sources within the British Army expect the counterattack to be 'decisive in ending this stage of the war and possibly the war itself'.